67

THE ETERNAL MALE

THE ETERNAL MALE

by

Omar Sharif

with Marie-Thérèse Guinchard

TRANSLATED FROM THE FRENCH
BY MARTIN SOKOLINSKY

DOUBLEDAY & COMPANY, INC., GARDEN CITY, NEW YORK
1977

B
Sharif

Published in 1976 as *L'Eternel Masculin*
by Omar Sharif with Marie-Thérèse Guinchard
Editions Stock
© 1976, Editions Stock

ISBN: 0-385-12541-0
Library of Congress Catalog Card Number 77–89418
Translation Copyright © 1977 by
DOUBLEDAY & COMPANY, INC., AND W. H. ALLEN & CO., LTD.

First Edition

Preface

What's he like?

For hours on end I questioned Omar Sharif in order to satisfy your curiosity and my own. I've always enjoyed taking the mystery out of myths and Omar Sharif is a present-day myth. Making him human with words was fascinating, and I've never been able to resist fascination or shrink from an obstacle.

And there were obstacles beforehand, since my myth was apparently trying to maintain a mythical image while not refusing to talk. The door stood open. . . . In the end we agreed completely about the way in which I would program his life, about how we'd collaborate in telling his story, over which he would be the absolute master.

Omar Sharif doesn't let everyday events sway him; he's in perfect control of his thinking and his actions. So much so that I was impressed at once by the spontaneity of his replies, which demonstrated the quickness of his mind. Talking to him is a constant give-and-take, a game of ping-pong. The answer is linked to the question without a pause for reflection or hesitation.

My second impression: the originality of his character. He doesn't copy others, he doesn't model himself after anyone. For him, life seems to be a game in which he doesn't participate. He watches it without being judgmental.

He relies solely on his own sensations, which comprise his mental world—an unusual world because it's a symbiosis of his Middle Eastern nature and his Western experience.

"I'm a Europeanized Middle Easterner," he loves to say. And that's the most accurate description of Omar Sharif.

An international personality in which the Middle East predominates, he readily identifies with those of his race, but at the instinctive level he's part of the Western world. He retains the refinement, the serenity, the altruism of the East while being receptive to the ideas and ways of the West.

His fatalism doesn't prevent him from being precise in everything, except where his past is concerned. Omar has few memories. He doesn't readily go back over the ground he's covered. Omar is a man of the present. He lives in an eternal present in order to renew himself.

He plays at life as he would at cards or dice, without counting the cost. His life is crowded with famous people, but they come and go without leaving a trace.

Omar is outside all the systems. He doesn't fall into any of their traps, not even the trap of ostentation. His living room, quite vast, is furnished with a long sofa, four chairs bearing directors' names, and a bridge table covered with a white cloth, which is used as a bar. Those are the star's only accouterments.

But—*is he a star?*

On the screen he certainly is, since his name appears in big letters on billboards; yet this "altitude" doesn't make him dizzy. He questions his performance constantly, he hates to go to screenings of his own films because he sees only their shortcomings (even the ones the audience doesn't notice), and that's the sole area of conflict in his inner self.

An anti-star star? Yes! He only commits himself professionally, but then he does so wholeheartedly, in keeping with his talent as an actor and always aware that everyone can improve. Too intelligent to play at being the "star," he prefers to play with ideas, a more subtle exercise, more in line with his psyche.

Physically, he's very handsome, and you know it and he knows it too, but he wins you over most of all with his intelligence, his depth, his offhandedness. Yet Omar gave me the impression of being very much alone in life.

To the question "Are you happy?" he answers:

"Outwardly, yes. Inwardly, lots of things are missing. . . ."

Who knows what he means by "lots of things"? He keeps lots of things to himself.

Marie-Thérèse Guinchard

1.

OBVIOUSLY, I'd never have believed it. Get to Hollywood and spend your first night in jail—that isn't exactly *obvious*. Especially when you haven't done anything wrong. When you haven't killed your father, raped your mother, pimped for your sister, or trafficked in narcotics. I'd landed in Hollywood with high hopes for newly won glory, having just finished *Lawrence of Arabia*.

It was in the wee hours of a morning in December 1962. Peter O'Toole and I were going to attend the grand premiere of our film that night. We'd prepared for that night, waited for it, day after day, for two years.

Heading toward Sunset Boulevard—the magic of those two words!—we went past a little theater where Lenny Bruce was playing. His run-ins with the law had done as much to make him famous as his talent. We went in. Out of curiosity? Looking for thrills? Don't ask me. But we loved the show so much that when the curtain went down we rushed backstage. Where was Lenny Bruce? The introductions were simple: "We may still be unknown but tomorrow our names are going to be heading the list of credits on *Lawrence of Arabia*." We told Bruce how much we'd enjoyed the show and invited him out for a drink. Before long the three of us were sitting at a table in P. J. Clarke's. By

1:00 A.M. Peter and Lenny were happier than usual. I wasn't as happy—I hadn't had as much to drink.

Lenny got up from the table saying, "I've got to go somewhere for half an hour. Do you guys want to wait here or come along?" We opted for the second and followed him. We'd hardly gotten into what must have been his apartment when he whipped out a hypodermic syringe, filled it with a clear liquid, and stuck the needle into a vein in his left hand. Obviously he was "on" something. The injection went slowly. With the needle still in him, he paced up and down. But his walking was abruptly interrupted by the ringing of the doorbell. Peter opened the door. The three policemen standing in the hall arrested us.

The seriousness of the situation restored some of the sense I'd lost in drinking. Being caught with drugs meant deportation and the frustration of all our plans. I tried to talk my way out of it, explaining how we'd come to be at Lenny Bruce's, drunk, at that hour of the night. Peter, completely soused, poured out a steady stream of invective against Irish cops. He couldn't stand the representatives of law and order. He had only abuse for them. At the time this was really annoying because he was systematically wrecking every argument that I offered in our defense.

My diplomacy proved ineffectual. Toward 4:00 or 5:00 A.M. we found ourselves at the police station. They searched us thoroughly. Nothing unusual in Bruce's pockets. Nothing in mine. In Peter's, an officer found pills wrapped in cotton.

"What are these?"

I knew them to be the innocent sleeping pills Peter always carried.

"They're morphine, damn you!" Peter replied.

That did it. All three of us were clapped into a cell. I had one last idea.

"Can I make a phone call?"

"Yes."

I called the Beverly Hills Hotel, where I knew Sam Spiegel was staying. I asked for his room.

"Mr. Spiegel doesn't want to be disturbed."

"It's very important."

Finally the switchboard operator rang his room. A sleepy voice:

"What is it? What the hell do you mean waking me up in the middle of the night?"

I came right to the point. "Sam, we're in jail—Peter and I."

From the other end of the line came a firmer voice. "What? In jail?" The prospect of his fourteen-million-dollar extravaganza coming out minus its two stars woke him up completely.

I repeated, "We're in jail."

"Why? What did you do?"

"They arrested us, with Lenny Bruce, for having drugs."

The great Sam Spiegel went into a panic. "Just stay put, Sharif."

He didn't have to worry about that—we weren't going anywhere.

Barely half an hour had gone by when he arrived, flanked by at least six lawyers. Very dignified men with hats and briefcases who immediately entered into a big conference with the cops. Well out of our range, of course.

The confab seemed to last forever. Finally a policeman opened the cell and said:

"Okay, you two can beat it."

Peter reacted quickly. "What? And leave Lenny in the clink? Then I'm not going!"

Peter had become pals with Bruce. When you're in the clink, you make friends easily.

"Don't be ridiculous," Spiegel said. "Bruce has a police record—they can't release him just like that."

"I don't give a damn," Peter retorted. "I'm staying with him!"

The seven civilians began filibustering with the boys in blue. It lasted quite a while and then they let all three of us go. The story never hit the papers, but it must have cost Sam Spiegel an arm and a leg.

The following day or, to be more exact, in the twilight of that wild day, the premiere was held—*my* premiere.

Peter, the blue-eyed Irishman who, in the guise of Lawrence, won England an empire, and I, the Egyptian promoted to Arab chieftain for the purposes of the film, were going to break the big barrier.

Together we entered a great sparkling theater. The jewels that enhanced the beauty of those superstars, stars, and Hollywood first-nighters! Elizabeth Taylor, Shirley Mac-Laine, Richard Burton, Gregory Peck were there. I recognized them—I, a guy who'd never laid eyes on them. They'd been the idols of my teen-age years and that night they became real! They congratulated one another, they smiled. I was an unknown, an Egyptian who prompted curiosity. But no interest. Not yet.

Peter O'Toole was no less a stranger than I to that movie world. Lawrence of Arabia was his first big role, just as Sherif Ali was for me. But our names appeared in big letters on the giant screen. Sitting in comfortable seats, we watched the audience for a reaction. It wasn't long in coming. Right from the start the spectators seemed spellbound. I felt the silence become gently oppressive. That first scene was silent—so was the audience. Lawrence, accompanied by a guide, has his eyes riveted on the desert horizon where a black spot seems to dance in a mirage; then the spot grows slowly, very slowly. Lawrence's guide runs to his camel. From his saddlebags he pulls a revolver, he takes aim . . .

and then crumples up. A shot has come from across the way. The black spot takes shape—it's Ali, the man who would become the friend of Lawrence of Arabia. It was I, the actor who'd been unknown five minutes before. The impossible had happened: a supporting role had boosted itself to the height of the leading one. A film had "discovered" two actors, had made two stars.

The running time was four hours. When the curtain came down Peter and I found ourselves the focal point of that theater full of celebrities.

We exchanged a complicit look, very quickly, and then we were separated. I felt myself borne off by a whirlwind. Elegantly dressed men and women came over to congratulate us. A sea of glossy mink and sable on undulating bodies carried me into a banquet room. I felt like Alice in Wonderland. Hollywood was mine, at least for a night; yet I still hadn't made the transition between the unknown actor who'd gotten off the plane thirty-six hours before and the person who was the toast of the town that night.

I'd come from my native Egypt to Hollywood to join Peter O'Toole. Yes, that's right—to join Peter O'Toole, because he'd forced that premiere on me. "If Omar doesn't attend, I don't attend."

The producer, who isn't exactly one of the smaller ones, had sunk a lot of money into this superproduction. He felt that it would be easier to launch it on a single name. Forcing two unknowns on the public at once might be a drawback.

In my naïveté, I'd sent a letter to the producer asking for the date of the first showing. He'd replied, "Don't bother coming—it would be inadvisable for you to attend."

That's when Peter stepped in and made them send me an airline ticket.

Out in the desert, we'd dreamed of that premiere. We'd be the heroes in a film that was going to captivate audiences. Our names would appear in big letters on the marquees of the leading motion picture houses, producers would besiege us with contracts, we'd have parts galore . . . our triumph was inevitable. Besides, my mother had predicted it and so had the fortuneteller.

I was thirteen years old. I'd been going to the English secondary school in Cairo for a few years. Periodically I acted in plays in the small theater there, thrilling my classmates with lines I'd learned by heart with all the confidence and conviction of a born ham. Maybe I wasn't much good but, carried along by my popularity with this audience of my own, I *thought* I was good.

Someone, I can't remember who, told me about a Greek fortuneteller who they claimed was infallible. Her reputation was enormous. She could see into the future of famous people, she advised them, she was never wrong. She'd become a legend in Alexandria. She gave readings at her home. By appointment only. Who could resist?

I dragged eight pals to Alexandria. There we were, standing Indian file before a small house in a poor section of the city. A woman who looked like a servant (and who turned out to be the fortuneteller's daughter) answered the doorbell and led us into an anteroom with whitewashed walls. We sat down on wooden chairs lined up along the walls. In the inner sanctum the magic cards would foretell the future.

Actually, we weren't terribly concerned about the future. We were happy in our own way and "tomorrow" was a word devoid of meaning. But adventures make you feel important; they take you away from the daily routine.

The daughter served us coffee, then the Greek woman appeared in the half-open door. She fitted the traditional image of fortunetellers: fat, with dyed red hair concealed by a kerchief tied at the nape of her neck, heavy make-up, a long dress with loud colors. She ushered in the first boy her gaze fell on.

It was Ahmed. Ten minutes later he emerged, beaming.

"She said I'll find happiness among many children."

Ahmed, a shopkeeper's son, had modest ambitions; he was satisfied with strolls along the boulevards, playing soccer with his friends. An easygoing fellow, he would enjoy family life. Did he ever become the proud father of many children? I have no idea.

The cards told Georges to be careful, something that worried him a bit. Had his effusive nature programmed him for reckless actions?

Amidou, a handsome, proud boy, got what he wanted: the fortuneteller said he'd be a Don Juan. He came out of the sanctuary strutting like a peacock.

And then it was my turn. There was neither a crystal ball on the table nor a parrot perched on the Greek lady's shoulder, only the black cat, sleeping on an old rug on the floor of a room furnished in rococo style. In the middle stood a square table where the Greek woman and I sat face to face. She didn't impress me, nor did the cards which nevertheless favored me.

"It's extraordinary," she said. "You aren't going to live in Egypt. You'll be famous all over the world. Do you hear—all over the world? And you'll make lots of money."

To be perfectly frank, I wasn't in the least surprised. I'd always known that my star would shine brightly.

They used to whisper around me that I was "an exceptional little boy." Naturally, this opinion was spread and maintained by my mother, who saw her son as a marvel.

They talked a lot about my gifts. At school I was the best

without (let's be fair) half trying, and it cost me a whipping
to fall below first place in the school one term. My mother,
who'd put me up on a pedestal once and for all, thrashed me
to avenge her outraged pride. She stimulated a gift for
learning within me that I hadn't perceived. At her call, the
new material seemed to surge out of a corner of my memory
where it could have remained dormant forever. This knowledge came to me naturally and stayed with me. I had no
need for memorization. I was learning that I could learn
without really working.

This didn't hold true for sports. I wasn't particularly well
co-ordinated. I had to make up for my meager ability with
long hard training. I exercised, acquired skills, and I made
the grade. I was becoming an athlete, just as I'd become an
actor by getting up on the stage in the theater of the English high school.

At the outset it was just a game, then an adult's game. I
would play at being someone else. I would act to thrill my
pals, and their applause said that I was on the right track.
The stage, perhaps the movies, would bring Michael Shalhoub out of the shadows.

Living in Egypt, a country cut off from the great Western
nations, seemed a handicap to me, but that's where my belief in fate and my break came in. "If they don't come looking for me, if they don't take me out of Egypt, it means that
my destiny must lie here. . . ." Yet something told me that
it lay elsewhere, something I was expecting. And it came.

So I stepped off the plane in Hollywood confidently, telling myself that the thirty years which had preceded this
evening had been nothing but a long preparation, a long
wait. . . .

A big American car stood there. Placed at our disposal by
the producer, it was waiting for Peter and me. So what if

there wasn't a uniformed chauffeur? Had we dreamed of a Hollywood like that? No, certainly not. We'd had plenty to do just visualizing the characters we were portraying.

For me, success was that Lawrence of Arabia, the man who'd been able to bridge the gap between two civilizations that I hold equally dear. Like Lawrence, that British officer-spy who, without repudiating his country, decided to become an Arab among the Arabs, I wanted to be a star among stars.

So when the greats of the movie world came after me in Egypt to accompany Lawrence on his long trek through the desert, it all seemed quite natural, believe me. I'd been expecting them, I'd known they were coming. They had come once before.

The first time was in 1956. I had just finished *The Blazing Sun*, my first Egyptian film, one that broke all box-office records. It should be pointed out that the leading role was played by Faten Hamama, the Egyptian idol. She would later become my wife, but I'll come back to that later. My professional memories are more coherent, more readily assembled than the images of my private life—so why not start with them?

Posters for *The Blazing Sun* were up on the billboards of several Cairo movie houses when an American team led by William Dieterle showed up in town. They'd come to film the exteriors for a biblical film entitled *Joseph and His Brethren*. (At that time the Bible was a main source of inspiration for movie makers everywhere.)

Rita Hayworth, at the peak of her career, was the heroine and her name on the billboard must have been enough, since the role of Joseph still hadn't been assigned. I would have imagined that it was essential. Yet, before hiring an actor for the part of Joseph, they were looking for his understudy. Producers grumbled about moving stars around unnecessarily. It was complicated and costly. An actor hired in Cairo would wear Joseph's clothes, provide his silhouette; the real Joseph, the one "made in Hollywood," would appear only in the close-ups filmed in the studio. In that way the producer saved time and money. He would come out ahead on the deal. Historical truth, local color—that was quite another matter. At any rate, getting back to William Dieterle, he saw my film and sent for me. Doubtless to entice me, his assistant told me that I had one chance in a million of playing Joseph from start to finish—not just the stand-in part that would be done along the Nile. The big *if:* if Hollywood liked the screen test I was going to do.

Still trusting in my star, I gave it a try. Then, as *The Blazing Sun* had been selected to represent Egypt at the Cannes festival, I left, delighted to make my first contact with the European movie world.

Jean Cocteau was the president of the jury. I'd seen his films at a Cairo theater that specialized in French productions. I admired him as an artist, I admired him as a poet, I admired him as a man who, to my way of thinking, could do anything and do it very well. I admired his aesthetic sense. I felt flattered just to be introduced to him.

He spoke to me in a friendly way. He told me—it's hard to repeat his words—he told me I was wonderful. He'd already seen *The Blazing Sun.* He declared that I was an excellent actor, that I had an interesting physique. He'd taken a liking to me, I think. . . . I was twenty-four. . . .

The regulars of the Cannes festival rarely saw films from the "underdeveloped" countries, to use the expression that was customary at the time. Such films were generally shown at small screenings in the afternoon. Jean Cocteau had *The Blazing Sun* scheduled for a gala evening, May 1, which is also the date of the festival of flowers on the French Riviera.

The décor was showy, the audience sumptuous. For a young man like me, it was fascinating. I took my first steps in a glorious, sparkling world. . . .

For the first time I was seeing film stars in the flesh; I identified with them since I was handing out autographs too. Your first autographs are exhilarating, like your first cigarette, or your first woman.

Maria Félix, at the height of her popularity, came over to me. She was beautiful, divinely beautiful. Daniel Gélin and Maurice Ronet didn't put on any airs. They didn't act like know-it-all, blasé elders; they shook hands with me, as with a friend. Of their own accord, they acknowledged that I had "some talent."

The film was well received by the jury. They actually debated the question of giving me the Best Actor award but finally decided against it. Still, I felt less frustrated now.

Back in Cairo, I found a cabled contract from Hollywood: I'd landed the part of Joseph. I felt invulnerable—but Eros was getting ready to play a bad trick on me. Rita Hayworth had fallen in love with the famous Dick Haymes and followed him to Mexico, deserting the film, which would be dropped.

My first break had evaporated. Was I bitter about it? Sad? No, not even that. My Middle Eastern fatalism told me that this break would be followed by another. And it was telling the truth. The "other one" came along six months later—in the guise of David Lean, the director of *Brief Encounter, Oliver Twist, The Bridge on the River Kwai,* and so on—the list was long. Every David Lean film had scored an international success.

He entered my life via the telephone.

"Hello, this is the Cairo office of Columbia Pictures. We're making a film in the deserts of Jordan about Lawrence of Arabia. We've still got a minor part that's unassigned.

Would you consent to having your photograph sent to Hollywood?"

"Why not?"

Ten days later another phone call.

"Sam Spiegel is in Cairo, he'd like to see you. Could you be at his hotel in a half hour?"

Since my childhood, I'd consumed every magazine, every trade newspaper, every column devoted to the movies that I could lay my hands on. I knew all about the great stars, their eccentricities. I'd also read up on the great producers and knew that Sam Spiegel was one of them. I knew that he could make or break an actor. Yet I went to that meeting without undue excitement. He, too, must be part of my destiny.

He greeted me in his suite, sprawled out on a couch, flanked by three assistants. The spitting image of the person I'd imagined on my way to the hotel: fat, important—yes, that was my first impression, he was important. He had a cigar in his mouth, an enormous cigar. He was the typical producer. I answered him in English. That impressed him. For an American, an Arab who spoke English fluently was a bit of an anachronism; that must have put a few trumps in my hand.

I spoke his language with a slight and undefinable accent, just as I spoke French, Greek, Italian, Spanish, and even Arabic. I spoke those six languages in the same way, with an accent that enabled me to play the role of a foreigner without anyone knowing exactly where I came from, something that has proved highly useful throughout my career.

Sam Spiegel watched me. I watched him.

"Would you like to do a screen test for a second part that we've still got to write?"

Three days later a small private plane dropped me off in

the desert where all I could see was a fence post, standing straight and alone. But soon the post moved and came toward the ladder. It was David Lean. He looked me over unashamedly, from every angle. Movie people have a nasty habit of undressing you with their eyes—I had to get used to that. Once the inspection was over, he put his arm around me and finally said something.

"Let's go get a costume."

We headed toward a big tent. To the wardrobe man who came hurrying over he snapped, "Go away, this gentleman knows what suits him better than you do." Speaking to me, he added, "What do you think of this black one?"

I picked a black djellaba. David Lean led me to the make-up tent.

He tried a beard on me. "No, that won't do." He tried a mustache on me. "That's it. What you needed was a mustache." From then on, it would be part of my characterization. Without being aware of it, David Lean had just changed me—at least, in my physical appearance. That wouldn't be the last time. He would have a preponderant influence over my career.

Meanwhile, he led me toward spotlights and reflectors that didn't give a hang about the sun, which, though shining brightly, seldom shone in the right place. Artificial lighting could be regimented more easily.

I spotted a tall, blue-eyed fellow. "Peter O'Toole," the director said. Peter was the typical Irishman. We exchanged a few words, just enough for me to pick up his sense of humor and his gift of gab. His speech was different from mine. I was counting on a meeting in terms of humor . . . I wasn't disappointed.

They had me do a scene with Peter-Lawrence. And then another with a French actor I was glad to meet again:

Maurice Ronet. Ronet had been hired for the part of Sherif Ali.

These screen tests were sent to America, along with an evaluation from David Lean: "As you'll see for yourself, the stand-in is a real Arab who can act." The answer came quickly. I wasn't going to get the "minor part that still had to be written." I was going to be Ali.

I've since learned the story of how I got the part that made my career. David Lean had looked all over the United States and Europe for "Ali, the Arab." He wanted an actor whose dark hair and eyes would contrast with Peter O'Toole's blondness and blue eyes. He wanted Ali to be true to life. A month before shooting was to start, having found no one who satisfied these requirements, he'd given Sam Spiegel carte blanche; Spiegel contacted Maurice Ronet, who signed a contract and then flew to Jordan. True, Ronet was dark. As for his eyes . . .

As soon as David Lean saw him he phoned Spiegel: "He won't do—he's got green eyes."

"It's too late," Spiegel replied, "he's hired. You'll just have to make do."

David Lean wouldn't admit defeat. He called his assistants. "Get me photos of every Arab actor—there's got to be one who's just right!"

That was when one of his assistants phoned me. That's how, having climbed the first rung of the international movie ladder in a minor part, I wound up at the top, alongside Peter O'Toole.

Peter's name still hadn't gone beyond British borders, while mine was unknown in both Europe and America. We often talked about the day when the Mecca of the film world would become ours. We'd never been to Hollywood.

We had, however, imagined it. We'd put together this vision on the basis of stories told to us by Alec Guinness, Anthony Quinn, and David Lean. They'd had time to talk, we'd had time to listen—we all lived under the same tent.

What a fantastic break—making my first movie with great actors who would share the same meals, the same worries, the same conversations!

When they work in the studio, actors are hidden behind the masks of the characters they're portraying. The day's work over, they split up until the next day. They seldom have a chance to get to know one another.

We, on the other hand, were living out in the middle of the desert. We were forced to watch ourselves live, listen to ourselves talk. . . . Actually, I watched them live, I listened to them talk. Thanks to them, I was entering a coveted world, the world of acting, of movies, of experience. . . .

We spoke of what they'd done and what I hadn't done, of what they'd seen and what I hadn't seen. From those talks I took whatever suited my own nature.

Peter O'Toole showed me tricks of the trade and the very next day I'd try to put them into practice. Arab film actors use lots of mime and grandiose gestures that come more from silent movies than talkies.

David Lean curbed my Middle Eastern temperament mercilessly. "He who can do the most can do the least," he told me by way of encouragement.

Thus Michael Shalhoub gradually became Omar Sharif.

I'd changed my name to do *The Blazing Sun*. I was born Michael Shalhoub. The name Michael annoyed me. Anybody could be a Michael. I tried to come up with something that sounded Middle Eastern and could still be spelled in every language. OMAR! Two syllables that had a good ring and reminded Americans of General Omar Bradley.

Next I thought of combining Omar with the Arabic *sherif** but I realized that this would evoke the word "sheriff," which was a bit too cowboyish. So I opted for a variant—I became Omar Sharif . . . and Omar Sharif I remain.

Alec Guinness spoke about Shakespeare, the itinerant player, the theater manager, the playwright. He spoke of the "god" Shakespeare. The English high school in Cairo had taught me only the cold lines of a playwright who'd been dead for centuries. "All the English actors," said Guinness, "deify Shakespeare. When they leave the drama schools they make their debuts in classical repertory companies. In England, classical repertory means Shakespeare. George Bernard Shaw runs a very distant second." Alec Guinness had managed to conquer his extreme shyness, his fear of people, his fear of himself, and offered incense at the altar of the Bard.

Guinness was the most timid actor I'd ever met. He broke through his reserve only to speak about his profession; he opened up only under the stimulus of acting. Perhaps he wasn't aware of it, but he undoubtedly stirred up the flame that was smoldering in me.

Very happily married and father of a son he adored, Alec had been through years of sorrow. His only child had been stricken by a very serious ailment against which medicine could do nothing. Guinness, who was Jewish, went from synagogue to synagogue to pray to the God of the Jews. In vain. His son seemed doomed. He prayed to Allah and Buddha in different temples. Nothing happened.

One day, doubtless by chance, he entered a church and bowed before the God of the Catholics. His son recovered and he converted to Catholicism. He became fanatically

* *Sherif*—denotes noble ancestry in a Middle Eastern country. *Trans.*

Catholic, fanatically devout. He could not bear to have anyone speak disparagingly about Catholicism in his presence. . . . He was an astonishing individual.

I got off on the wrong foot with Anthony Quinn. A minor
incident spoiled our relationship right from the first day of
filming. We made up, later on, during the shooting of
Behold a Pale Horse.

Anthony is a strange being, perpetually at war with himself, traumatized by his half-Irish, half-Mexican ancestry.
His early days on the screen typecast him in Indian parts,
whereas he wanted to escape from that world, which he'd
known all too well through his mother. He wasn't liberated
from it until he married Cecil B. DeMille's daughter.

His personality asserted itself and his talent developed
. . . but the wound never healed completely. He remains
taciturn, withdrawn, although his intellectual energy is
great. He needs to be doing something constantly. He
draws, he paints, he writes poems or a book. Anthony is
quite gifted, but he disperses his talents in trying to express
himself in too many areas.

David Lean and Peter O'Toole talked nothing but movies.
Peter is the very stereotype of the ham; he's a big man in his
own life—that's part of his profession. He represents an astonishing caricature of the Actor with a capital A and,
what's more, of the Irish actor. In Peter's native land, an
actor has to drink a lot, get into brawls, dress in a way
different from others. Peter drank, brawled, and dressed
with a great deal of originality, maintaining the traditions of
the Abbey Theater actors of his childhood. Gradually he
made up a character and wound up by believing in it. I can
safely state that Peter's inner self is not the one he lets people see; rather, he thinks and acts naturally like that other
self.

He is like a prism that reflects the seven colors of the spectrum in a splendid rainbow. Peter the actor would identify readily with the scarf of Iris, the messenger of the gods; an actor on the set, he's also one in everyday life.

I've heard him tell a particular story a number of times, a story we'd lived through together. It was extraordinary. Each time he would embellish it until he made it into a perfect story, transforming it to suit his audience. He would strike out any part of it that hadn't gone over with his previous audience, expand the attractive parts, and always call me to witness: "Isn't that the way it happened, Omar?" I would acquiesce, I'd become his accomplice; the story was a tall one, but so well told that I'd try to believe it myself. Peter believed it simply because the story was beautiful and produced the desired effect. With it, he captivated his audience.

I recall an innocent adventure that took a bacchanalian twist.

While *Lawrence of Arabia* was being filmed, on one of those wild trips we took to Beirut every month, I woke up in a strange apartment, in bed with a girl. I'd lost all notion of time. I didn't even know if it was night or day. I suddenly got the feeling that our plane had flown back to the desert . . . and we'd missed the take-off.

I stumbled around the apartment and in another room I found Peter asleep in the arms of a girl nearly identical to the one I'd just left. I shook him awake.

"What day is it?" I shouted.

"I dunno," he replied laconically.

"I have a hunch we're supposed to be on the set!"

"Really?"

I urged him to get dressed. I did the same and we rushed to the airport. "The plane left yesterday," the man at the

check-in counter told us. We chartered a plane. The cast
had been shooting without us since the day before.

It was only an incident but with each telling Peter added
two, then four, then six girls in our beds. The innocent night
of two men who'd had too much to drink became an orgy.
The day we'd missed became a week, and Peter told it wonderfully.

Movies, dramatic art—that was his world. Take him outside show business and he knew absolutely nothing. The
happenings of everyday life were foreign to him. To discuss
them with him was like talking to a child. But as soon as you
spoke of a "dramatic situation," he became a genius, because
acting was something innate with him, his one mad passion.

I never knew him to have any hobby except dancing the
twist and he seldom felt like doing that.

While we were still in the desert we prepared for our re-
entry into civilized life. A magazine (I don't know how it
turned up in our tents) informed us that a new dance was
becoming the rage: the twist.

"We're going to look like hicks when we get back."

"That's right. What can we do about it?"

"Learn the twist!"

We had a teacher flown in from Paris who began his
working day when we finished ours.

He showed up with one single record in his suitcase:
"Peppermint Twist," by Joe Dee at the Peppermint Lounge.
It was played until late each night. We trained, first taking
turns with the instructor, then dancing with each other.

The grooves of the record wore out one by one but the
same class was held every night. Under the tent in the middle of the desert we danced until we were exhausted.

Our monthly trips to Beirut enabled us to try out our
newly learned skills and when, eighteen months later, we

landed in London, we were past masters of the twist . . . which had gone out of style.

We soon got over it.

David Lean had that same cult of the métier and the same apathy toward anything that might take him away from it. But his character was diametrically opposite from Peter's. From his Quaker parents, David got Puritanism, religiousness, and a lack of humor, but also their integrity, their philanthropy.

David was fascinated by the sky and by everything there that he saw (or thought he could see). I've seen him, out in the middle of the desert, stop filming so that he could watch a high-flying plane disappear over the horizon. He just couldn't take his eyes off it. He was also fascinated by rockets and anything connected with space.

His austerity showed in his behavior, in his work. He was also shy, which didn't fit with his excellent physique.

At the time we were shooting, in 1961, David was a youthful fifty; now he's in his sixties but doesn't look it. He has an extremely powerful face—a piercing gaze, an eagle's nose. He really has the profile of a bird of prey. He's a terribly attractive man.

His supreme pleasure isn't making films but, rather, observing the audience's reactions. He goes to see his films incognito. He takes a seat, watching for a tear, a smile, or a movement. If the audience isn't in tears at the precise moment he's anticipated, he makes note of it: "I was wrong." Then he corrects his work, rewriting the faulty script. He works in some music, adds a few frames before or after, shortens or lengthens.

For David, laughter or tears comply with strict mechanisms: they result from a precise convergence of forces that

must bring the audience to a certain emotional pitch, either
happy or sad.

If all his films have been successes, it's because he's made
them in accordance with these criteria, gearing them to his
audience. "My one joy," he says, "is having an audience."

He reworks his reels with the prodigious skill of the film
editor that he was before becoming a director.

David reads a great deal, but he reads what might be
made into a film. All his reading is connected with his film
making. The first selection is made by agents and writers
who send him scripts.

We were bound by a community of interests, but a more
fraternal feeling bound me to Peter O'Toole, and this close
friendship was what actually made *Lawrence of Arabia* a
success.

The scenario was adapted from T. E. Lawrence's book,
Seven Pillars of Wisdom, though it follows Lawrence over a
period of only two years, which he spent in Jordan and
Syria.

Some of Lawrence's writing fascinated me. I learned
whole passages by heart. Speaking of military uniforms, he
wrote, "This death's livery which walled its bearers from ordinary life, was sign that they had sold their wills and bodies to the State: and contracted themselves into a service not
the less abject for that its beginning was voluntary." He also
noted, ". . . the effort for these years to live in the dress of
Arabs, and to imitate their mental foundation, quitted me of
my English self, and let me look at the West and its conventions with new eyes: they destroyed it all for me. At the
same time I could not sincerely take on the Arab skin: it was
an affectation only. Easily was a man made an infidel, but
hardly might he be converted to another faith. I had

dropped one form and had not taken on the other, and was becoming like Mohammed's coffin in our legend . . ."

A great deal has been said about the nature of the Lawrence-Ali relationship and countless articles have been written about it. The screenwriter did not expressly define their intimacy. He presented their complicity. It revealed itself throughout the film in affectionate behavior, which was actually a reflection of the everyday life that Peter O'Toole and I were living. The moviegoers must have been aware of this. I'm convinced that the fraternal feeling that sprang up between Peter and me was one of the great things to come out of the film, just as it made those two years in the desert two years of joy, two full years.

Actually, everything about that film was extraordinary. The performance was exceptional. Hollywood could never afford a production on that scale nowadays.

In order to avoid any trace of footprints, David Lean had chosen to shoot the picture in a part of the desert remote from roads (the nearest was a hundred and fifty miles away). Our sets had to be absolutely virgin and so did the horizon. The tents were set up twenty miles from the place where we were shooting. We were supplied by one of three planes available to the production; however, our water was hauled in by tank trucks.

The cast, the technicians, the Bedouins represented about a thousand people to be fed and cooled off, inside and out. Makeshift showers (collective for the Bedouins, individual for the acting and technical people) were set up near the tents. The showers operated by means of a cord that opened a valve.

The camels and horses, hundreds of them, had to be watered and fed. Almost as many people were required to implement the logistics of the production as were involved in the actual filming.

Our tents were equipped with air conditioners and refrig-
erators. Servants assigned to each actor and each technician
watched over our comfort. They did our laundry, made sure
that cold drinks could be served to us at any hour.

A restaurant operated under the direction of a master
chef from London. His wine list was nearly as impressive as
the one at Maxim's. And the barman mixed drinks like an
expert. A ping-pong table stood in the room next to the bar.

On Saturday nights there was a holiday atmosphere in the
canvas town. Movies were shown outdoors for the entire
crew. And nobody missed roll call. But don't ask me what
we saw during those 102 shows—102!—I wouldn't be able to
name one title. I used to look at the screen without seeing it.
I simply enjoyed the anachronism of a world I'd forgotten,
of some impossible plot in the solitude of the dunes. I enjoyed the incongruity of voices that seemed to come from
the beyond, there in that incomparable silence which nothing disturbed—not the stirring of leaves, the singing of birds,
the buzzing of insects, the sound of footsteps, or the murmur
of a brook.

The outside noises to which I'd been accustomed in city
life suddenly meant something to me because they had been
stilled. Had I ever really listened to them?

My life, until I found myself in that remote corner of Jordan, had been only a succession of landscapes, places where
people and animals lived together. And there I was under
that canopy riddled by little fireflies, subjected to the uniform desert, obeying its law, its magic. There were a thousand of us and yet I was alone, face to face with myself. My
mind had been trained by my French studies in what is
called Cartesianism, but in the desert my Islamic atavism
surfaced.

The mysticism born of the desert took hold of me and the
more I tried to deny it the stronger it grew, until my resist-

ance broke down: I experienced religious feelings for the
first time. I thought about Fénelon,* I felt myself yielding
to mysticism through a heightened state of awareness
created by that atmosphere and by my imagination. I experienced what I'd thought to be mere legend when I was a
child.

In my home, my father had come to wake me each morning; first he would speak some gentle words, then he would
begin a wrestling match which I would soon take seriously
and which invariably ended with a victory for me.

I've since realized that the outcome of our "fights" was decided even before they began. Fatherly love made that con-
cession to the child who already imagined himself a man
and a conqueror.

Vanquished, my father would be obliged to pay a fine. He
had to tell me a story and that was how, gradually, the legend of the desert took shape for me.

The Arab's character, my father used to tell me, had been
forged among the dunes where he pitched his tent. The desert, he explained, made man a grain of sand among the
other grains of sand. It made each person part of the others,
just as the individual particles of the minerals formed sand.
Hence the Arab's dependence and, also, his generosity.
Hence his sense of hospitality and the offhandedness of his
relations with others. Hence his spirit of fraternity and his
aggressiveness toward anyone who doesn't reply to his over-
tures.

My father described the desert as a frightening place
where men were at the mercy of thirst and hunger, a uniform infinity where one can leave a trail between sky and
sand only at the cost of long and often painful experience.

In the desert man is alone, without protection. In a city

* François de Salignac de La Mothe (1651–1715), French prelate and
writer. *Trans.*

he has a roof, a house in which to take shelter. He generally has water with which to cool himself off, to wash himself. He has a water bottle that he fills by turning a tap when it becomes empty.

In the desert men have only their individual resources—their courage, their resistance. They have only the hope of reaching a water hole and the shelter of a tent on their long trek. Away from an oasis, death stalks their tracks, men drag death with them, fall prey to it.

In this, the desert is terrifying and terror leads us to meditate. It is no accident that so many prophets came from the desert. There they found faith, a philosophy, a God. They identified with that one God, protector of the solitary man, and that God engendered monotheism. All prophets preached the same religion and called upon the same fraternal precepts that are found in Islam. Later on, men interpreted and adapted God's word to suit themselves.

Islam! This Arabic word means "resignation" and codifies, all by itself, the law of the desert. The man of the desert is resigned to thirst, resigned to hunger, resigned to death. Mohammed, in teaching men that death isn't an end in itself, spared them the fear of dying.

"The Arabs have no fear of death, since Mohammed then takes them to his side," my father used to tell me. Through the verses of the Koran and the Bible, he taught me always to have hope.

Under the starry skies, feeling like a grain of sand among the grains of sand, facing the big screen that was supposed to be a link with cities, with the so-called civilized world, I would think about my father and, like him, I believed in God.

Did the other members in the cast fall under this same spell? Did they experience the desert in the same way? I often thought so.

At any rate, David Lean had chosen to live like a Bedouin. He lived in a trailer at the very place where we were shooting the film.

Every morning we would be waked at five-thirty and we'd go to his trailer. And every morning we'd see the same sight: planted in the midst of that trackless immensity, a chair bearing a man's weight. It was David Lean studying the horizon, impregnating himself with the setting that he would give to the adventure of Lawrence and Ali. He'd already been there, motionless, for two hours. He had to have his ration of the desert every day.

It was unforgettable—the sight of that man seated alone, in the middle of dunes undulating into infinity.

The arrival of the team would put an end to his contemplation. He assembled the cast in his trailer and spoke to them for a long, long time—three or four hours—about the scenes that were to be shot. He would explain how to play them, the idea that he had of each character's reactions to a situation he'd studied down to the last detail.

Meanwhile three hundred Bedouins, wearing sandals muffled with wool, were erasing all trace of our footprints, from one end of the horizon to the other, with broad palm fronds.

Toward noon, we'd rehearse. The sweepers of tracks would move in once more, then again after each rehearsal, and . . . the setting sun would bring us back to camp and David Lean would return to his contemplation.

The following day he'd give his instructions to the technicians before shooting the sequence rehearsed the day before, once, twice, ten times, fifty times if he felt it necessary. Once, twice, ten times, the Bedouin sweepers shook their palm fronds.

That's why the filming of *Lawrence of Arabia* lasted two

years. Without women—well, almost. Actually, we were forbidden to have any female company.

So we lived seven hundred and thirty days that way—just
men—and without bathtubs. . . . No, I'm exaggerating. We
lacked women and bathtubs twenty-eight days a month.
Once this period had expired, we were entitled to a forty-
eight-hour break to use as we saw fit. Anthony Quinn and
Alec Guinness devoted themselves to pleasures of their own,
the nature of which I never tried to determine. Peter
O'Toole and I used to go to Beirut, two or three hundred
miles away.

A small plane flew us there in two hours. Our program
was always the same: on arrival, we would plunge with
delight into a bubble bath. Only those who have been
deprived of a bath will understand what this means.

Washed, rubbed down, we would then set out to digest the
desert. We used to put bottles of champagne in our bathtubs, which were filled with cracked ice. Then we'd store a
case of champagne in the trunk of the car that ferried us
from one bar to another, our only poles of attraction, and
we'd drink without stop for forty-eight hours—always in female company, of course. Like sailors at the end of a voy-
age, we'd always look for the most sordid night clubs—the
ones around the waterfront. We felt an overpowering urge
to go slumming. The desert had nothing impure, so that's
what we needed. We went hunting girls in every bar, every
night club, to make up for the restrictions placed on us by
our producers.

Relaxed, we would return to our Jordanian tents and
plunge back into the Hollywood dreams that filled a good
many of our evenings.

With a taste of mead on my lips, I saw the invitation and
was ecstatic. Mrs. Vincente Minnelli, one of the women who

ran fashionable society in the motion picture capital, had invited me to a party. The ones she gave were listed in first place in the annals of Hollywood. Clearly, Mrs. Minnelli, a ravishing Yugoslav, had boosted me to the first rung of stardom by sending me her card.

At the time Hollywood was dominated by a few women who classified actors. These women set up three kinds of parties—the first reserved for superstars, the second for declining stars, and the third intended for "unsorted" ones. Dishrags are never mixed with napkins. So Mrs. Minnelli's party was first class—with me as the main attraction.

She phoned her close friends and, to make sure everyone would attend, she said, "It's going to be fabulous, my dear. The Egyptian will be there—you know, the good-looking fellow with the mustache who played the part of Sherif Ali in *Lawrence of Arabia*. The Irishman will be there, too, he's got those beautiful eyes, I'm sure you noticed them."

New stars were the only distraction in these closed circles, whose habitués yearned for thrills, for the exotic at home. These "inaccessible" people, among whom I would henceforth belong, turned up their noses at public entertainment.

Obviously, I accepted Mrs. Minnelli's invitation right away because I must admit I was flattered, I was delighted, and because you've got to play the game. . . . And the prospect of rubbing shoulders with famous people was extremely attractive.

The same thing happened on the days that followed. Invitations came from well-known producers, script writers, directors. Their wives were very lovely and so were the other female guests. I had lots of fun at these parties.

On these occasions I did my share of flirting, like everyone else. But don't expect me to enumerate my affairs. I neither want to mention them nor have the right to do so. Gallantry forbids my doing this and the conjugal (or simply romantic) futures of my random partners makes discretion a duty. I don't think any man can derive glory and benefit from being the husband or lover of Omar Sharif's ex-mistress. I don't know how a man would react if he read that his wife had had intimate relations with somebody who's in the news, but when two people meet they both have the right to be silent about the past which they alone know.

Furthermore, I don't think I've reached the age to write my memoirs. I'm only at the halfway mark and I still live in the movie world where most of my love affairs blossomed. So . . . everything connected with the personal area must remain secret if I value my human relations, and I most certainly do.

Romance can't be bought and sold. To divulge certain aspects of my private life would make me feel as if I were selling something. So I'll only give a faithful account of those few liaisons I wasn't able to keep up.

Having said this, I can mention some extraordinary parties thrown by public relations agencies which, it must be said, abound in Hollywood. Every day I'd get albums of photos of ravishing girls, along with an "instruction sheet."

"The girl that you select will be your companion tonight at the Coconut Grove, a fashionable night club, and the check will be on us."

These lovely ladies were young actresses. An evening spent in public with a star could do more to promote their career than years of study at drama school. The press, tipped off beforehand by the P.R. men, sent out photographers who snapped the star and his "date" from every angle. The next day the newspapers were full of articles that spoke of the "budding romance."

Between cocktail parties, I would readily agree to play that game. Why not? It helped me and it was fun. I needed the press myself, and I managed to bring a few starlets out of obscurity this way. From time to time I'd see some of them on the screen, never in starring roles, always bit parts, which wasn't so bad.

A good film makes you a star, entitling you to the best tables in the best restaurants, to the respect of rich and poor alike. A bad movie makes your standing go down; people snub you and the good tables are reserved for someone else.

Studying the customers of a fashionable Hollywood restaurant will reveal each one's standing. I've seen big stars relegated to the far end of the room because, that very day, the bottom had dropped out of their success.

So I went to Mrs. Minnelli's party. It was held in a succession of drawing rooms opening onto the inevitable swimming pool which decorates every Beverly Hills bungalow worthy of that name. In fact, when you fly over that community it looks like a placid sea spawning not plankton but exotic plants and buildings painstakingly copied one from the other.

I was living, I was seeing everything I'd ever read in those columns that I'd devoured at fifteen. I marveled at finding everything just where it was supposed to be.

In the middle of that stereotyped amalgam, I was a thing rather than a person, but the rules of the game demanded amiability. The sacred cows asked me stupid questions about Egypt: "Do you always go around on camels there?" or "Do you always wear Ali's costume?"

Among themselves, they spoke of nothing but movies. Each one boasted about the merits of his latest film. I sensed in these conversations more hopes than realities.

I'd been confronted with a civilization that differed greatly from mine, yet I was very much at home.

Human contact has always been easy for me. Middle Easterners are warm by nature and friendship plays an important part in their lives. This promotes relations between people. In that respect, I'm a Middle Easterner.

I don't think I have enemies; if I have any, I don't want to know who they are. And I think that my receptiveness to others, no matter what the level, has been an important factor in my success.

2.

IN 1962 MY COUNTRY was living through the Nasserian era. The Suez Canal had been nationalized. Israel was allied with France and Great Britain. Accordingly, Jews were out of favor with Arabs and vice versa. In the movies, in the American press, Jews were numerous and powerful. I was an Arab. What was going to happen? Would they boycott me? Would all doors be closed? Nothing happened! The Jews adopted me. They made friends with me. With me—who'd never denied my loyalty to Egypt. Great tolerance reigned. It was natural for me: I'd always stayed far away from any feeling of racial discrimination or anti-Semitism. Hadn't I belonged to a minority in Egypt? Hadn't I been born a Catholic in a Mohammedan world?

Oh, of course, this difference had never made itself felt in any tangible way. Neither my family nor I was ever subjected to any cruelty, baiting, mental or physical persecution. But as a member of a minority, I'd had the feeling of not being like the others. When you're in a minority, you stick with your own. It's a matter of self-defense. I was no exception to the rule.

Furthermore, dual religions (or any other dualities) never appealed to me. I believe in men rather than in God. I was in the United States, among Americans. They excited my curiosity. Did these men and women live in the same way as I or didn't they? That's what I wanted to find out. Questions of race and religion didn't matter to me.

I might as well say it, the United States disconcerted me. Especially its women . . . And yet they weren't at fault.

I found America disconcerting because it was unlike any other country. It represented a world in which I was out beyond my depth.

I'd learned to think and to live in a certain way among people who had much in common, who—to varying degrees —resembled one another, mentally and physically. Everyone had something within him that his neighbor possessed. And then all of a sudden I was transplanted into a world in which everything was foreign: its emotions, sensitivity, weaknesses, ideals, vices, envies, malice.

America has its own values. I discovered its energy, whims, vitality, unparalleled technical prowess, its ways of storytelling, of seeing, its very special optimism, its characteristic selfishness—namely, self-glorification which colors all of its feelings and allows the self to experience them intensely. I watched its way of being, its way of living, and I failed to understand.

The self-confidence, superiority, and independence of the women! These very beautiful women whom I wanted to seduce and, perhaps, dominate. These women so different from the ones I'd known. These women who dared to breathe without the artificial lung of the male! Who dared to assert their will to be!

Although I'd been given a French education, I felt like a Middle Eastern male. Or was it the image I had and still have of the submissive spouse? In my country, women are dependent. They blush. And I like that. I'm used to that. And in this country, which I was seeing for the first time, a woman who blushes is considered a naïve country girl. Politely, but a politeness tinged with contempt. I couldn't love a woman who couldn't or wouldn't blush! I didn't wonder if they weren't sometimes playing a game—*I knew they were!* Curiously enough, American women didn't blush. Was I to blame?

What kind of country was this where women seemed to be in a position of strength? Good God, that struck me as contrary to nature! The world was a man's world and would always be a man's world, where women had their place. . . . But what if that weren't true? Then what about history? What about the history being made today? Mightn't the roles, which had seemed so well cast by nature, be inverted?

I knew about the women's liberation movement and that American women had been the first to throw off the yoke. How could I fail to respect any attempt at consciousness, any search for identity? I should have admired them. And I did. But how could I admit it?

I was a Europeanized Middle Eastern man. It was asking a lot to make me be an Americanized Middle Eastern man as well. Asking too much, perhaps.

I should have remembered that the word "liberty" appears in the Declaration of Independence, between "life" and "the pursuit of happiness." This document, of course, applies to everyone, both male and female. And American women contributed to forging their nation's history as much as their men did. That's why they were respected—and respectable! But they have also been placed on pedestals just as mothers are in other societies. Let a woman enter a room and all the men get up. If she comes up to a table in a restaurant a man will always be there to offer her a chair. These outward signs of deference astonished the Middle Eastern male that I was. It's said the American woman is a luxury and, in a country where everything is for sale, she's the one who does the buying.

Advertising on billboards, in the newspapers, on TV, is aimed primarily at her. But aren't the Europeans headed the same way? Of course, with a slight time lag, as with everything that comes from America. Let's just say that the beautiful American woman was able to assert herself before her sisters abroad and that I went to the United States ten years too soon. I just wasn't ripe!

Likewise, the tempo of American life disconcerted me. That, too, reached Europe, then the world. But in 1962, I thought that my American friends didn't know how to measure their time—neither time to make money nor time to live. They were extraordinarily efficient, I thought then; they had a wonderful knowledge of practical things; but they knew nothing about so many useless but beautiful things. If I'd brushed up on U.S. history I would have remembered that the idea of success via the dollar had been inculcated in them by an evangelist.

At the beginning of the century a Philadelphia pastor had traveled the country singing the praises of work and its just recompense—money.

"Getting rich," he said, "is an honorable ambition. Money is power, and every man and every woman should struggle for power in order to use it wisely. I say this to all: Be rich, be rich."

That pastor said that at six thousand meetings and, in so doing, earned nearly eight million dollars. Many Americans must have listened to him because those good principles were instilled in their children.

And yet, with the passing years, the situation has gradually changed and the children of those Americans are going to play great roles. They've gone beyond their borders. They've been forced to do it, furthermore. Americans put their faith in other strong currencies: the Deutschmark, the Swiss franc. They've got to fight for oil, that sublime substance, which they control all over the world. The dollar can no longer buy everything. The system has been shaken. Their Constitution, rich in admirable principles, has been flouted.

The United States had deified money; now America may realize that the dollar is no longer "the boss."

Man has regained his footing, he has developed a new taste for certain life principles. . . . We always come back to them!

3.

THE EGYPT OF MY CHILDHOOD was miserably poor, but Egyptian poverty didn't leave me traumatized. There was something almost happy about it; the people could smile through it all. At least, that was my impression.

I was born on April 10, 1932, under the sign of the ram, with a Libra ascendancy. My birthplace was Alexandria . . . amazing Alexandria where there are so many reminders of the men who have passed through there over the centuries. No doubt that's what makes me uncomfortable in young countries.

Alexandria, with its luminous tower that lighted the harbor of Pharos. The lighthouse, the "tower of health."

Alexandria, heir to Hellenic civilization. With its library, its six hundred thousand volumes. All the learning of the world on papyrus scrolls. How could this have failed to mark my life? Walking in Alexandria or roaming around the Bronx as a child won't make you the same person. I'm a son of Alexandria. Of that Alexandria where subterranean galleries were tunneled to lead the water of the Nile into the palaces where it arrived purified; meanwhile, the people had to content themselves with cloudy water, which was the source of incurable diseases.

I learned later on that the Egypt of Farouk wasn't much

different from what it had been for generations. A mere two hundred families—between fifteen hundred and two thousand persons—held the national patrimony. They measured their wealth by the time it took a train to cross their property. They used to say, "Mr. So-and-So is six-hours-by-train wealthy," or "Mr. So-and-So has only four hours' worth."

The So-and-Sos comprised three or four generations that had clung to the family mansion, producing wives, children, uncles, aunts, cousins, of the first, second, and third degree.

Their "people" clustered in mud huts that also sheltered farm animals on cold nights and in bad weather. Their wages were miserable—the equivalent of twenty dollars a month. While purchasing power was relatively high (a pie filled with beans cost only one cent), the poor rarely had enough meat. They contented themselves with two or three of those bean pies each day. That filled their bellies but left their bodies ill equipped to stand hard manual work and resist epidemics.

Once a year there was a festival marking the end of Ramadan. The people would feast on roast lamb and chickens. They were very poor, in the sense given to the word by Western middle-class societies. Living in my privileged world, I scarcely realized this. They seemed to live their poverty in happiness.

My father was (and still is) a prosperous timber merchant. He led the same life as the other well-to-do businessmen, primarily Lebanese-Syrians. An easy life.

He belonged to the same clubs as the big landowners. We were totally assimilated—with one exception: we were Christians, they were Mohammedans. Money did the rest. It opened all doors. And the doors that counted were those of three clubs. Very exclusive, British-style (founded by the British, what's more). There was the Royal Sporting Club,

*Omar Sharif
making his First Communion.*

With his parents.

*With Faten Hamama,
his ex-wife,
and his son Tarek.*

Bridge championship.

Omar Sharif and his horse Royaltex, winner of the Prix de l'Europe. AGENCE RECOUPÉ

The yearling sale at Deauville. AGENCE RECOUPÉ

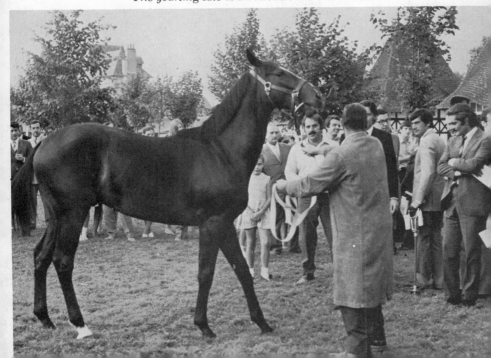

With Mrs. Boris Schapiro and Vodka. TREVOR HUMPHRIES

With Anouk Aimée. ROBERT FRÉSON

which lived up to its name with golf courses, cricket fields, and squash courts; the Royal Automobile Club, where the financial elite dined with music; and the Mohammed Ali Club, which was more like a circle.

And here we must mention gambling. The Egyptian's reputation for being a gambler isn't exaggerated. This fact was well known in Monte Carlo, where they used to roll out the red carpet whenever some Cairo VIP landed with his entourage.

Every night the gentry would surround Farouk at the Mohammed Ali Club. The stakes were enormous, even at the conquian tables. (This game, not unlike rummy, is played with forty cards.)

The games of chance brought together people divided by political games: the English, the monarch, the leading Mohammedan families, Syrian and Lebanese businessmen, Catholics and Jews. All money smelled the same.

In that colorful crowd there was my mother, an inveterate gambler. My father's financial situation improved and so did our social standing. Mother was delighted—mainly because, with each deal, with each rung on the ladder, she could gamble more and more. And this woman, who wasn't really snobbish, who was generous and kind, began consorting only with the elite, since only the elite gambled.

I can see her now. She was beautiful by the standards of those days. She looked like the actresses of the 1930s. Of average height, well built, her greatest charm lay in her long, naturally red hair. She'd had to pay for the splendor. Like all real redheads, her face was covered with freckles. When she was young she'd tried to have them removed. A beautician had helped her with the job. Each freckle burned off left a scar that gradually faded away; at the time, however, she'd been terribly upset.

Mother was elegant, charming, interesting. She was seductive and knew how to use that asset. She always managed to come up with the right word, the right way of holding herself, the right wink.

Father was very tall and slender. He must have grown stooped because now he seems to be of average height. He used to stand a shade over six feet. I'm only a half inch shorter and have never given the impression of being tall. Perhaps it's a matter of bearing. He used to be dark, but now his hair has turned white. He was slim; now he's grown heavy, paunchy. He used to be termed a handsome man. He was also a good man, and still is. Good as gold—to his family and to everyone else.

Father having been raised by friars, Mother by nuns, my parents were very united, like all deeply religious people who have strict family and social moral codes. They weren't very well read. They were plain, religious people who could neither do nor think evil. I've never heard my parents make a critical remark about anyone. My father was an extreme case, moral rectitude personified. A brilliant businessman, he never stooped to underhanded tactics. Mother was shrewder, more cunning, terribly crafty. So she and I had a problem. Even as a child, I always knew what she was thinking. She knew this and wasn't particularly pleased.

In Alexandria we lived in a small, two-story building surrounded by a garden. It stood very close to the beach, in a district called "Cleopatra by the Sea." I've since returned there. My old house was still standing, just as it looked in my memory. It hadn't suffered the weathering of time; at any rate, it didn't seem to have aged.

My first years went by happily, uneventfully. My parents reared me rather strictly, but spoiled me. They refused me nothing and, most of all, they gave me a great deal of love, oceans of love.

I was four years old when my father decided to move his business to Cairo. He wanted to get even with a Japanese earthquake.

His father, my grandfather, had four brothers, one of whom had settled in Japan and become rich there. Extremely rich. He was a bachelor. In 1923 a terrible quake shook the Japanese archipelago. Afterward, under the wreckage of his house, there were found—along with his body—chests full of gold.

In the interim my grandfather had died. His brothers shared the treasure chests, forgetting their sister-in-law, my father's mother. The poor woman, alone, utterly unprotected by the law, which at the time sneered at females, was cheated. Yet she'd amply deserved her piece of the pie. Her husband had been in a wheel chair for seven years (gangrene after a nasty insect bite cost him a leg). She'd never complained about that invalid husband or their unruly sons. When she died my father, the eldest son, was fifteen. "Take care of your brother," she'd told him.

He obeyed, giving up his school career. His brother (my uncle Henri) has a diploma from an engineering school in France.

But my father never forgot the story of Japan.

That reminds me of an unexpected visit I received in Deauville, France. A gentleman introduced himself to me, saying, "My name is Habib-Deloncle. Aren't you the grandson of Aunt Afifa?"

"That's right, my grandmother's name was Afifa and her maiden name was Habib."

"Then we're cousins."

We spoke for a long time about the family's "woman saint," as my father called his mother.

At the time, Habib-Deloncle was a member of General de Gaulle's cabinet.

They say that everyone has a guardian angel. Mine was named David Lean.

One month before shooting was finished on *Lawrence of Arabia,* when twenty-three months had sealed a friendship based on trust, respect, and admiration, when we knew that the film would be a hit, David told me: "The day this film comes out, you'll be a star and you're going to face a great danger: people are going to offer you parts like *Son of the Sheik, The Eagle of the Desert,* and that sort of thing. You've got to turn them down, all of them. I know the appeal of money is strong. To force you to build your career, I'm going to lend you money, lots of money. Every time anybody makes you an offer, remember that you owe me money and you'll be forced to reject the stupid offers."

David Lean did, in fact, lend me money and I deliberately turned down the silly roles, the ones spawned by producers or script writers trying to exploit Ali's popularity. I eliminated many absurd parts that way. Not all of them, unfortunately. I signed a contract with Columbia without knowing what I was getting into.

This event (and it was an event for me who'd just been thrust into the international movie world) took place at the London office of that prestigious company, after the desert sequences of *Lawrence of Arabia* had been shot. Columbia placed great hopes in the film and therefore had every reason to want to keep me on their payroll.

Having been sent for, then ushered into a huge office, there I was, face to face with the boss. Just he, with no agent there to protect my interests . . . or his.

He began amiably by appealing to my vanity: he had made me into an international star and my career promised to be long and fruitful. Then he handed me papers to sign. Did I really read them? No, because if I had the main clause in that contract would have struck me. It tied me to Columbia for seven years at a miserable salary.

For seven long years this company had me making films that I wouldn't have chosen otherwise. For instance, *Genghis Khan,* which obliged me to spend four months in Yugoslavia for a ridiculous fee.

Lawrence of Arabia won eight Oscars. My stock shot up and I got lots of offers. David Lean stepped in—even then. He phoned his friend Fred Zinnemann, the director of several big films: *High Noon, From Here to Eternity,* et cetera.

"Do you have a film coming up? I've got an excellent actor for you."

So Fred Zinnemann put me into the cast of *Behold a Pale Horse* with Anthony Quinn and Gregory Peck. A likable fellow, Gregory Peck was extremely good-natured and, something rarely found in those circles, even-tempered. I played the part of a big Spanish priest who had to choose between a charitable lie and the truth that killed—in short, a very human role.

The film didn't get the public's wholehearted support, but David Lean was casting for *Doctor Zhivago.* He offered me the lead. Only he wasn't making it for Columbia, so they had to work out a deal. I had to bear the expense. Columbia "rented" me to the company making *Zhivago*—in other words, they set up a new contract and paid me only the fee provided for in the old contract binding me to Columbia. So they got the profits, while I established my reputation.

Doctor Zhivago was actually a turning point in my life. But I must go back to the past before rounding this bend.

When I hitched myself to my star that first month in the spring of 1932, my father wasn't a wealthy man. He just earned "quite a bit of money." I first saw the light of day in a family with an average income . . . a family that was going to prosper.

It wasn't easy for businessmen to make profits in those days and my father, like the others, played the game, asserting that "business was business" and had nothing to do with religious feelings. That's how he soured me for the business world and anything connected with it.

Father showed his generosity outside his business where, as he used to say, he couldn't be philanthropic or he'd lose his shirt. He was undoubtedly right, but each person must act according to his own conscience. My sense of fair play differed somewhat from the rules of business and, I must admit, I had doubts about my father's honesty.

Moving the business and our family to Cairo marked an event. A modern twelve-story building was our first residence, then came a more luxurious apartment and finally a very elegant house. My father was becoming a wealthy man.

Europe was at war. The Allies were readying plans for the Normandy invasion. The economic repercussions made themselves felt in Egypt, where timber prices underwent the general fluctuations. Timber was scarce and, as demand must yield to supply, my father found another source of profit. He also salvaged for almost nothing (or free!) barbed wire that the British had strung around their camps during the desert fighting. He "cleared" land of this barbed wire and converted the stuff into nails: little nails for shoes, medium-sized or big nails for all purposes, and these nails went for high prices. He reaped huge profits.

Once again we moved—this time into Cairo's most fashionable quarter, Garden City, on the Nile. Our new house stood right between the British and the United States embassies. Our lucky days were beginning.

I knew about this social climbing. I heard it said at home that Father was earning lots of money while Mother spent more and more at the gaming tables. She even decorated our house in the style of the fashionable gambling casinos. She would invite her "cardshark" friends home between sessions at the clubs. King Farouk was one of them.

I remember him at our home—a gigantic, rather ill-mannered man. He'd had the misfortune—at least, I think of it that way—to come to the throne at sixteen, after the death of his father, Fuad I. He'd been given an excellent education but fell into the hands of corrupters and dilettantes who pandered to his weaknesses, hoping to win his favors.

A boy of sixteen can't resist temptation. Corrupted in his turn, Farouk lost all authority and he scarcely had enough time to satisfy his desires, as whimsical as they were. Invited home by my mother, he began to eat, left the table to gamble, came back to the meal, played again, then ate some more.

At times he compelled my mother to smoke a big cigar. My mother didn't like tobacco and he knew it; he seemed to enjoy making her cough. He cheated, everyone knew it, but they all had to pretend not to see. Protocol was excluded from these card games for the King's entourage. They would call Farouk "Your Majesty," but that was as far as it went. They had to give in to his whims.

My mother told me recently about her first game of cards with the King. One night she was gambling at the Club Mohammed Ali, as usual. Farouk was seated at a table quite a distance from hers but she could see him from her table. Absently, she noticed a short confab between the King and his secretary, Pulli Bey, an Italian, then saw the latter coming up to her.

"His Majesty requests that you play a game of poker with him," Pulli said.

"I'm sorry, but I can't match His Majesty's stakes."

Pulli Bey relayed this to the King, whom my mother watched from a distance. Soon afterward she saw my father bow before Farouk, then come toward her.

"Go play with the King," he told her simply.

"But his stakes are too high!"

"No. I'll explain later," my father insisted.

That was her first card game with Farouk. She never told what the price had been, but she gave me my father's explanation.

Farouk had called him over and said, "We've run a check on your finances. You've got substantial accounts, so your wife can get into big games. I want to play with her."

From that night on she became his mascot and our house became a gambling den. Farouk would come over, bringing along his partners who were also friends of my mother. If the King said play—*you played*. He decided who would play against him and who would play on his side. And always men. The only exception: my mother. Because she was his mascot.

Extremely superstitious, Farouk wouldn't sit at a baccarat table unless my mother sat on his left. He would only start the game when she was there to cut the cards. He would win more, he used to say, when he took the hand after her. As a gambler, Farouk didn't like to lose.

Two games of cards stand out in my memory.

During one of my father's business trips to Europe, Mother played her daily game at Farouk's side and she was having a bad night.

"Your Majesty, may I stop playing?" she asked her august neighbor at the table.

"Why?"

"I'm losing six hundred pounds. I can't go beyond that while my husband's away."

Farouk, who suspected everyone of lying to him, called the cashier over.

"What's Mrs. Shalhoub's account tonight?" Farouk asked.

"Majesty, Mrs. Shalhoub has withdrawn six hundred pounds from the bank."

Smiling, Farouk turned to my mother and told her, "That's funny. You were telling me the truth."

Then he told the cashier, "Put that six hundred pounds on my account."

He hadn't made my mother a gift—he forced her to go on playing in a game at which he was the big winner.

The other game took place in Alexandria where my mother was vacationing; the King was staying at his Montase palace.

Each night the sessions went on until late. Mother was exhausted. One night she decided to go to bed early. She told the desk clerk at her hotel, "I'm not in for anyone." She was awakened from a sound sleep by the ringing of the telephone.

"Hello, this is His Majesty's secretary. He's waiting for you in the lobby. The King refuses to start the game without you."

"I'm very tired—I need some rest."

"I've got orders to bring you to the club. The King's car is waiting for you."

My mother yielded to the royal whim. Once the game had ended, Farouk, who drove his car himself at night, paid my mother the "honor" of escorting her to her hotel, driving along the city's boulevards at a speed Mother can still remember. Weaving in and out, the King floored the accelerator, and his passenger's fright gave him an added thrill.

Mother has another strange recollection.

It was during a poker game at our house. She sat facing the King and, by chance, his eyes met hers. "Oh, so now

you're at it too!" he exclaimed angrily. "You're trying to see
if I have a glass eye!"

He paused, broke out in loud, deep laughter, then added,
"Well, for you, I'm going to take off my glasses, but I'm taking them off once and for all, so that you can shout it from
the rooftops—*I don't have a glass eye!*"

There were rumors going around that he'd had an eye put
out in some accident. That was why he always wore dark
glasses, people said.

"He had very beautiful blue-green eyes that were perfectly intact," Mother affirmed.

My father wasn't addicted to games of chance. At most,
he would devote an occasional evening to backgammon, a
very popular game in the Middle East. He preferred hunting to cards and had the privilege of shooting game on the
King's lands.

He got this favor through a friend, a Greek gunsmith,
who was in charge of hunting on royal property—mainly for
ducks and doves. Farouk seldom took part in the hunt. His
late nights out made this impossible.

As a rule the hunters waited for the royal blessing before
shooting and, as a rule, a messenger would bring His Majesty's orders: "Hunt, don't wait for me."

It should be noted that the doves, migrating from Europe
to the Sudan in the fall, fly over Egypt at daybreak. To be
precise, they fly directly over the palace gardens. Why this
particular piece of air space? No doubt because the gardens
are so close to the sea and because of their immensity. The
vast tracts of land bordering the Mediterranean were all
posted with notices bearing the royal seal.

Those who weren't invited by the court had to rent space
near outbuildings from which they could shoot doves or

quail. My father turned up his nose at quail: "They fly too low. But doves fly high enough to make it interesting."

Sometimes I'd go along with Father, who tried to show me the joys of hunting . . . in vain.

I'd just entered the English secondary school—I was ten. At that age, which my mother considered crucial, I was fat and awkward; I seemed to knock over everything I touched.

Mother was uneasy. She wanted her son to be tall and slim; she wanted him to be perfect, mentally and physically. So she decided to sign me up for the English school where sports were the thing. (At the French friars' school, sports simply hadn't been part of the program.) As though I'd been handed a magic wand, I traded hours of boring classes for hours of play. Compulsory but fun. Those fifteen-minute recreation periods in a tiny schoolyard were over. Now I bounded over the carefully tended turf of a soccer field. I had five such fields at my disposal. What a thrill to enter the world of manly competition! I'm convinced that my life would have been completely different if I hadn't gone to the English school. Sports turned out to be a decisive factor in my adult life.

I fell in love with soccer and became a good player . . . and I slimmed down. The weight melted away. At thirteen I was everything my mother had wanted: tall, slim, straight. It came to be taken for granted. Along with other things. The English school turned Michael Shalhoub into Omar Sharif.

Sports were compulsory. From among the leisure activities that we could engage in, I picked dramatics. I made a great discovery. The school's theater group gave me the keenest pleasure of my teen-age years.

The ham in me was already coming out. I was thrilled at the idea of being on stage. All my classmates were in the audience. I knew everyone out there and they all knew me.

The audience showed that they liked me. They congratulated me because I'd had the nerve to get up on the stage.
I grew confident. I was becoming the actor who would
someday conquer Hollywood.

4.

I WAS ACCEPTED IN HOLLYWOOD but I never felt like living there; I never chose to live there. I liked it for three months, because the weather was good, because I had a fine house there, because I had a pool, because I was having fun. For three months . . . after that it began to bore me.

Three months. That's how long it takes to shoot a film in the studio. And in Hollywood work in the studio takes place under extremely comfortable conditions. You've got all the time you want when working. You move among depersonalized people without having the impression of being depersonalized yourself.

And yet, when I create a character, I almost become an automaton in the hands of a good director. I play the part he asks me to play. My creativity begins at the point where I take a hero who up to then has existed only in a script and make him come alive. I draw this character from deep within me, but the director is the one pulling the strings. And he's also the one who, at the outset, gives the character a soul which he explains to me and which I've got to grasp.

Lawrence of Arabia was my big creative thrill, because for two years I was Ali night and day. The part fitted me like a glove. There was no gap between Omar Sharif and Ali; there was no change from studio to home. They were blood brothers. And at night Sharif didn't leave Ali and go home—they slept in the same tent.

That film was shot from start to finish without stopping. Just as in a play. I was Ali until the curtain came down.

The atmosphere I found in Hollywood was a bit like that. The movie capital deserves its name. You live there in test-tube conditions, in a vacuum. You never quite get away from the movie you're shooting. That's what I love about Hollywood. And that's what I hate about Hollywood once the shooting is over.

So I love Hollywood and I don't love it. Instinct? Logic? I don't know. There's one thing I do know for certain: every time I've had a choice between a film to be shot in the United States and one in which the action takes place in Europe (preferably France) I've always picked the European one.

I had a French education, as I've already said. I'm a Middle Easterner who thinks like a Frenchman, thanks to my French uncle.

I was six when he came into my life. He was a teacher of French in Cairo. He was the husband of my mother's sister (whose eyes are the same color as mine). He and my aunt made a perfect couple, being well matched physically and emotionally. They both had generous natures. She was small; he wasn't very tall. . . . Now they've grown even shorter, but their hearts haven't changed.

My uncle is eighty now, my aunt fifteen years younger. He can scarcely see any more; her eyes are still keen. But he's the one who reads the newspapers every day. He's still just as fond of bridge and crossword puzzles. And his interest in current events still keeps him glued to the television set.

The years weigh heavily on him and his life has become humdrum, but his mind is intact. I still get the same pleasure talking to him, which happens fairly often since he followed the family's migration. He settled in France with his two sons, my cousins, who have done quite well for themselves. The eldest runs a large construction company that puts up big hotels, ones like the Hilton and the Sheraton. The younger one is a kinesiotherapist in Narbonne and follows the town's rugby team very closely. Both cousins are about my age. We get together every now and then at their parents' home in Cachan and it takes me back to my childhood.

From the time I was six, I spent my vacations at my uncle's. He'd been through World War I and used to tell me about it, as well as about France between the two wars.

He loved tennis and his idol was a player named Henri Cochet; he made me love Cochet and tennis. My uncle loved bicycle racing, a sport completely unknown in Egypt; he got me interested in bicycle racing.

He loved poetry. During meals he would recite verses with tears in his eyes; he gave me his love for poetry.

My uncle loved to read and selected books for me. He showed me the wonders of Alphonse Daudet. First I'd be *Tartarin sur les Alpes*, then *Les Rois en exil*, then *Le Petit Chose*. Daudet's *La Chèvre de Monsieur Séguin* enlightened me on the dangers of freedom; *Le Secret de Maître Cornille* showed me the value of well-placed pride. A proud man was respected by everyone. The antics of the *sous-préfet aux champs* kept me in rapture for hours.

Later on my uncle introduced me to the works of Jules Verne and Anatole France. I understood the French language so well that I read the English writers—even Shakespeare—in French. I laugh to think of it today. At the time it seemed perfectly natural. I wasn't at all interested in Egyptian literature.

And it was also my uncle who made me aware of painting and drawing. He told me about painting just as he'd told me about World War I. He filled me with a deep love of France. I even got to the point of being "charmingly chauvinistic." I preferred Racine to Shakespeare because Racine was French.

My parents and their friends also spoke French, but they didn't speak the same language as my uncle. I took refuge in his home, which was humble compared to my father's, but I learned about another world, a different society. My parents lived well but weren't concerned about intellectual matters. At my uncle's, I had the feeling that I'd left a flashy, showy world to find the light. I wasn't questioning my parents' generosity or honesty. They knew this.

When I was eight my uncle took me to a French film. It was the great era of Marcel Carné and Jacques Prévert, whose films, as far as I was concerned, couldn't compete with *Lives of a Bengal Lancer, Four Feathers* or *Tarzan*. At the time I believed in everything I saw on the screen. I couldn't separate fiction from reality. I was held spellbound by the adventures of Errol Flynn, Gary Cooper, and Cary Grant . . . and yet, after that first French film, I would wait impatiently for Mondays, the day they changed the program at the French moving picture house.

On Mondays, I'd get my weekly ration of French film art. It didn't occur to me at the time that the French could turn out anything but art. On the other days of the week we'd go to see American films. The fact is that I became an actor in Egypt before I'd ever seen a film made in my country. I didn't see an Arab movie until, having become an Egyptian actor, I felt the need to see what the others were doing.

At fifteen I left for France. Finally I was going to see my uncle's country.

Each year Monsieur Normand and his wife, a young couple residing in Cairo, would organize a summer camp for French children living in Egypt. It was 1947. My cousins were going on the trip, so my uncle signed me up to go with them. I was traveling by ship for the first time. That baptism really excited me.

We went down the gangplank in Marseilles and began our tour of France, which took us through the Alps, the Pyrenees, Normandy, Brittany, Alsace. To my amazement, France was even more beautiful than my uncle had described it. No doubt I retain conventional images of it, but no others have supplanted them.

The Alps and the Pyrenees fascinated me with their valleys overlooked by lofty white peaks. People explained to me that that immaculate coat was made of accumulated flakes called *snow*. I'd never seen it before. The Pyrenees enchanted me; they seemed to offer you their suspended glaciers and blue lakes.

In Normandy and Alsace the countryside was less striking than the thatched and peaked roofs of the houses, so different from our own. Unfortunately we never got to stay in one—our group was put up in camps, but those camps left a deep impression on me. That was where I fell in love for the first time.

She was in our group. Tall, slim, and pretty, she was French (what's more, from Britanny). And like any good Breton, she had inherited that Celtic and Viking fondness for long voyages. She had the courage to make them. She wasn't like the other girls. I really fell for Yane Le Moullour. Her eyes were as brown as hazelnuts; her hair had the fragrance of honey and its color as well.

A very innocent, very sincere relationship grew up between us, one that would last for years . . . but I still didn't
know about that.

I was sixteen and I knew I'd be an actor. I passed the first
part of the exam for my *baccalauréat* degree, then the second. The exam papers were to be graded at Oxford, so my
diploma would be valid in England. I was more than a little
proud when I got it. High marks from the Oxford professors
had opened the doors of the leading British universities.
There was just one hitch—I didn't feel like continuing my
education. This despite the fact that my teachers claimed I
had a gift for math.

I was eighteen and formed an amateur acting group. I
picked French plays. Anouilh. Why Anouilh? Why not Mo-
lière or Racine? Because I had so little money. I had to elim-
inate the classics since they called for scenery and costumes.

You see, for my sixteenth birthday my father had given
me a new car as a present; he paid all my bills in the bars
and night clubs frequented by hopeful young actors like me;
he told me to go out and have a good time—on him. But he
refused to encourage my aspirations for the theater. To him,
it was a passing fancy, a whim that would keep me out of
his lucrative timber business.

The story of that first car shows what my relations with
my family were like.

One of my father's friends, a wood importer like him,
went to Paris for the Automobile Salon with his wife. He
bought her a Simca, a turquoise coupe with elegant lines.
The car created a sensation back in Egypt, being the only
one of its kind there. Naturally, I would have given my eye-
teeth for that Simca.

How could I get it? Ask my father? That was risky. He
gave me lots of things, but he didn't like whims and that's

exactly what he would have called this. On the other hand, Mother could never refuse me anything.

"Mother, your friend Asma has a terrific car! I'd give anything to have it. Please, I want it!"

"But the car belongs to Asma. And she must want to keep it."

"She can buy another one. I want it."

"*You want it*. That's easy to say, but you can't make Asma sell it to us. . . . Hold on, I've got an idea. Her husband is a close friend of your father's. I'll talk him into making an offer for the car."

My mother's influence on my father was as strong as my influence on her. Father did go and see his friend. They argued. Finally the man seemed ready to give in, but his wife had gone back to France for a few weeks.

"I can't make any decision on this while my wife's away."

My father came home sheepishly. Somehow, the more trouble we had getting the car, the more I wanted it.

"Mother, you're more diplomatic. Go see Asma's husband. I'm sure you'll get him to sell."

My mother phoned Asma in France. She spoke so convincingly that I got the car of my dreams.

Six months later I wanted a different one and my father—through my mother's intervention—gave in to this new whim.

But he wouldn't have any part of my acting career.

For lack of funds, I had to get the members of my theater troupe from the French school and from the Jesuit fathers.

I handled production and played the leading roles. As I've said, I had grown tall and slim. The English school had done a lot for me. I'd learned to think quickly and had gained self-confidence. I understood this when girls began taking an interest in me. I said to myself, "Good, everything's going to turn out all right."

My physique proved to be a real asset. People are more apt to accept someone with a good-looking face and a well-made body than a person whom Nature has cheated. I'll even go one step further. It's often said that beautiful women are stupid. That's not necessarily so. But beautiful women seldom have to make an effort to be liked. Everybody raves about the cute little baby, then they shower attention on the beautiful girl, and finally they admire the ravishing woman. Why should beautiful women knock themselves out trying to be bright or good company? They become lazy. People get lazy when they're good-looking.

We rehearsed here and there, whenever a social gathering emptied some houses and filled others. When there was a cocktail party at one of my friends' homes or at mine, we looked at the list of guests. We could always find an empty drawing room for our rehearsals. For the last three or four rehearsals I rented the university theater, where we put on our plays. Just three or four performances, no more than that. There simply weren't enough French-speaking people in town.

Once, when I had a year and a half's experience, I decided to put on *Eurydice*. I invited the French ambassador, Monsieur Couve de Murville, to the opening night. He congratulated me during the intermission. My father was in the audience. His paternal pride had been so flattered that I knew he was ready to give in. The newspapers spoke highly of my directing and emphasized my acting ability.

The years went by. I was in London. Unknown. *Lawrence of Arabia* hadn't been finished. We'd just left the desert. We weren't going to start shooting again for two months. Then we'd be working in Spain, at Almería and Seville, in

Spanish-Arabic palaces which were supposed to be ones in Damascus and Cairo. Subterfuges are part of the movie game.

But Sam Spiegel insisted that I follow the rest of the cast to England. The idea of my going back to Egypt worried him. I might get into an accident or some other situation that could prevent me from leaving again. After all, the producer's money was at stake. He had to protect his interests. So I lived those two months under his guardianship, which certainly was relaxed. I felt right at home because I was used to the English way of life. I'd learned it in Cairo classrooms. I'd learned it again in the desert with Englishmen . . . and Peter O'Toole became my guide in London.

We spent our evenings and nights together, doing all the pubs and night clubs. One night Peter broke with our tradition. He decided to take me to the theater. That represented a first for me. The foreign plays I'd seen in Cairo had been performed with makeshift scenery and actors who were out of their element. I had lots to learn.

And I went, determined to compare the performance of these British actors with my own. I put myself in the place of the actors and, to my delight, saw that they were using the very same techniques. I recognized my own moves, gestures, expressions. I didn't have to be ashamed of anything I'd done on that little stage of the Cairo University theater. In fact, I was vain enough to compare the world's best acting to my own. . . . Well, that's youth for you.

That evening was my introduction to the English theater. I found it fantastic for its stagecraft and its actors. Today, as I look back, I have the feeling that the English actors had already streamlined their style at a time when bombastic delivery was still standard for the repertory in other countries.

The main attribute of British actors lay in their training in the field. Whether an actor came out of drama school or not, the procedure was always the same: walk-on parts, then minor roles in repertory before any big parts, but every evening he'd be out there on stage, facing an audience. That's the best school, the only one.

Instead of repeating the same lines, making the same moves, gestures, expressions for six months, the actor gets into the shoes of twenty characters. In France this is the privilege of a handful, those hired by the Comédie-Française. What about the others? Night after night they have to play the same maid, the same ladies' man, the same grande dame, the same tough guy. Every night the same character. That is, of course, if their play doesn't fold. Then there's always the danger of being typecast in one role and you can have a devil of a time getting back out.

Actually there are two kinds of theatergoers: the French, who treat themselves to an evening at the theater, a bit like champagne on New Year's Eve; and the English, who are born with a love of the theater. British people go to the theater the way Frenchmen go to the movies—after coming out of the office or factory at the end of the day. Shows start very early in England. I don't know if these customs have shaped the character of the people or vice versa. But this fact has enabled Englishmen from every social class to rub shoulders at that sacrosanct place, the theater.

I was also in London when they held a special screening of *Lawrence of Arabia* for the Queen. Noblesse oblige. The producer was an American but the director and Alec Guinness were Her Majesty's subjects. And of course Lawrence had been an officer in the British Army.

I wasn't being deceitful when I spoke of the grand premiere in Hollywood, which was actually the second world premiere. But I put it in first place because the producers' reactions in the movie capital were more important for me than Queen Elizabeth's reactions (no offense to Her Majesty intended).

So there I was, standing in line with my fellow actors. At the end of the picture the Queen passed us in review. A few friendly words to each of us and the ceremony was over.

The picture had a tremendous impact on the moviegoing public. A producer offered me a part in a film with a brilliant cast: *The Fall of the Roman Empire* with Sophia Loren, Alec Guinness (again), and James Mason. Being Sophia Loren's husband for six months was a tempting prospect, but it was only a supporting role. I weighed the pros and cons. I didn't feel like going back to Cairo, and on what I was getting from Columbia I couldn't have gone on living in Europe without working. And then I wanted to be in closer touch with movie people. So I took this part that brought me to Spain and made me miss my father's visit to London. He wanted to see his son's "extravaganza." Afterward he told me about standing in line for two hours to buy a ticket. He stood on line six days straight to see his son in the role of Ali six times.

Meanwhile, I reached Spain.

Sophia and I—that was the meeting of two Mediterraneans. We got along fine from the start. We became good friends. For six months I was her closest friend, somebody new in her entourage and—what was important—I played poker and—more important—I let her win. Sophia adored poker but hated losing. Every night we got into a game that didn't end until she won. Oh, just small sums, the stakes were never high.

At first I thought her Neapolitan honor prevented her from allowing her adversary to win—even at the card table.

I soon realized that the Neapolitan code of honor had nothing to do with it. The real reason: she was a bad loser, *period*.

Our card games were nevertheless pleasant and playful; I enjoyed spending a few hours with her privately or with her friends. Because Sophia's professional life in no way interfered with her social life. She was a perfect hostess who entertained company or played cards with the same pleasure. In her home. No matter where she was making a film, she'd have a villa or an apartment. She couldn't live without a home. She isn't the type for hotels. If Sophia hadn't been born poor she might never have chosen to be an actress. She would have been perfectly happy at home with a husband and a raft of kids. Family life is her real vocation. The birth of her children meant more to her than her biggest screen successes. I'm sure of that.

Sophia led the life of a middle-class housewife. Certainly her stardom made it hard for her to go out, but I'm sure she didn't like night life. What did she really like? Inviting friends over to try the Neapolitan specialties that she cooked herself: spaghetti, macaroni, lasagna, and eggplant. And did she know how to make them!

On the set she was very nice with her co-stars. She became more demanding with her director, forcing him to be careful with his camera angles, because she was obsessed with her *nose!* Like all the stars, she tries to defend her profile. Sophia isn't the only woman to have thought her nose was too long. What about Cleopatra's nose?

She'd dream up these little imperfections even though she's very beautiful. She embodied all the criteria of beauty . . . in tall women. Personally, I prefer them smaller. That's more in line with my idea of femininity. But I don't claim to be one of the high priests in the religion of female beauty.

With Princess Anne, at a film showing for the Queen. CENTRAL PRESS PHOTO

With Camilia Sparv of Mackenna's Gold, P.I.C. PHOTOS

First Egyptian film.

Lawrence of Arabia.

Dr. Zhivago.

With Julie Christie, in Dr. Zhivago.

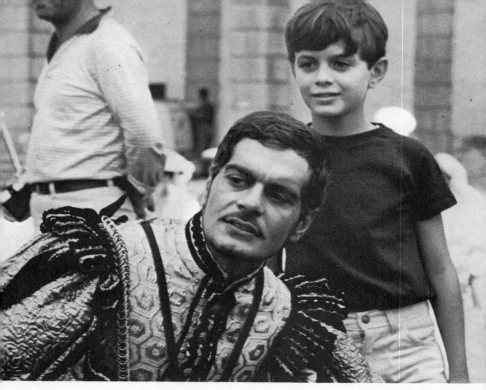

Tarek visiting the set during the shooting of La Belle et le Cavalier. *He is eight years old.*
TAZIO SECCHIAROLI

Tarek now.

Sophia Loren was my first European co-star. Our marriage on the screen went no further.

This wasn't the case with my Egyptian co-star, Faten Hamama, the national Cinderella.

I was twenty when Jusef Shadine, a director who learned his trade in the United States, asked me to take a screen test for his forthcoming movie, *The Blazing Sun.*

Jusef Shadine was a boyhood chum. We'd been in the same class at the English school. We belonged to that same Christian-Lebanese world. Our paths seemed to diverge when he left for the United States to study movie technique, but I met him again in Cairo a few years later, still just as friendly. I bumped into him by chance—well, that may not be true. There was every likelihood of our meeting, since we moved in the same circles.

So he was readying *The Blazing Sun* and gave me a screen test, which he liked. Then it was just a question of convincing the leading lady to play opposite a beginner.

She invited me to her home for tea. Point-blank, she asked me to give her a sample of my acting. I got a brainstorm: I launched into *Hamlet* in English, knowing full well that she didn't understand a word of the language and would never admit it. She listened attentively, or so it seemed to me, and that's how I got my first movie contract . . . by a trick.

Jusef, on the other hand, didn't leave anything to chance. For eight months he had me reading plays—Shakespeare's most of all. He felt they had every possible shade of expression.

Finally the big day came when I was ready to face the camera and the crew, who welcomed me as a friend of the director. Right away I was one of the family—I never had to experience the trials and tribulations of a beginner.

Jusef Shadine, a graduate of the Pasadena Playhouse,

spoke the language of the international movie world. He had nothing in common with the Egyptian movie makers, who were ingenious but inexperienced. What's more, he had a brilliant career. One of his most recent movies, *The Bird,* produced in 1974, had a tremendous impact. Banned in Egypt at first for political reasons, it was shown abroad—notably in France, where it scored a huge success. Then the movie hit the marquees in Cairo when the ban was lifted.

So I had my start with a master director. I was *his* discovery. The shooting went off nicely. I might even say it went off very nicely. My parents reconciled themselves to the fact that I wouldn't be in the timber business. They'd just regained their serenity when tragedy struck.

One night, as they were leaving their club, a man came up to tell them that my car had been found abandoned a few miles outside Cairo—with a bloody shirt on the back seat. My mother was so upset that she didn't feel the cigarette between her fingers (I later saw them with third-degree burns).

The car had been found on a deserted road. My parents drove out there and found my car and the bloodstained shirt. Terrified, they went back to Cairo and made the rounds of the police stations. At our neighborhood station house they saw me sitting at a table with the desk sergeant, a cup of coffee in front of me.

My mother rushed up to give me a hug.

"My son! You're alive! We saw a shirt full of bloodstains. Did someone hit you?"

"Shirt? What shirt? Oh, that. The shirt I was wearing on the set today. Don't worry, that was just red dye for the scene we were shooting."

"But what about the car? Why did you leave it out there?"

"I got stuck."

"Then how did you get here?"

"Somebody saw my car and the dyed shirt and they ran for the police. While the whole force was out looking for my body, a couple of policemen picked me up at a night club and brought me here. They realized that there was no need for an investigation."

On the set the atmosphere was pleasant and I got on well with Faten Hamama. In order to follow the script, she consented—for the first time—to be kissed on the screen.

She never allowed herself to be seduced in a film. Her audience would have been embarrassed, even shocked. Every one of Faten's fans considered her his own and the producers respected the public's sensibilities. They played on them.

The kiss she gave me was quite innocent. I had fainted and Faten's lips merely grazed my own, but the reporters were there. The best-known members of the press published the photo of the kiss. That touched off a huge scandal.

Overnight I became the sacrilegious man who'd dishonored the idol. Every Egyptian felt outraged, deceived by that kiss—which was like manna for the producer. The film broke all box office records for an Egyptian production. There were lines a block long in front of every movie house. But I was practically banished from screens in my native land. No producer would have dared to hire "the man who caused the scandal."

Between Faten and me, this story created a rather equivocal situation. We had to avoid each other, which wasn't easy because we moved in the same circles, went to the same places. When a mutual friend invited one of us over he had to make sure not to invite the other. When Faten and her husband were in a public place, somebody would come and tell me to stay out of there.

And then one day we bumped into each other in a restaurant that I'd just happened into. I was sitting at my table, Faten came over to say hello, and all the forks remained poised in mid-air. We'd been living in dread of meeting out on the street and there we were, face to face, in public. Both of us were overwhelmed by the fatality of that meeting and we became obsessed by it. She began thinking about me all the time and I could never drive her face out of my mind.

This untoward meeting gave a more daring director the idea of putting us together on the screen again. Rumors of an affair began circulating; at first they were rather embarrassing, then they drove us into each other's arms. In the beginning it was only an affair. Faten had a husband and daughter. Then our liaison became an idyll. We finally decided to get married.

Her husband gracefully consented. It should be pointed out that in Egypt at that time the contract uniting a man and a woman was a unique document. The holder of this paper was the husband, who retained all rights and could compel his spouse to respect every clause. If he so desired, the husband could simply deny the existence of any commitment. The woman had no tangible evidence of her marriage.

Faten's husband was a real gentleman. He tore up the contract and, to authenticate the separation, went through this formality before the authorized official.

We could be married, but there was still the religious problem. I was Catholic. Faten was Mohammedan. One of our religions would have to be given up. For Faten, idol of the Mohammedans, that was impossible. I had no choice.

I went to the government office where a man wearing a turban sat behind a desk.

"If you want to become a Mohammedan," he said, "repeat after me: 'I believe that there is only one God.'" After which he added, "'I believe that Moses, Jesus, and Mohammed are the prophets of God.'" The man in the turban then said, "Put your signature on this line." I signed, after denying that Christ was the son of God, and I became a Mohammedan. It was as easy as that—at least, officially.

Informing my father of my religious treason was something else. I had good reason to be terrified. I still hadn't forgotten my Protestant girl friend.

It's something that still means a lot to me.

Yane Le Moullour had been my fiancée for six years. You remember the ravishing tow-haired girl I met on that summer trip to France? She's the one.

I used to think I was fated to marry her. We followed each other very closely right from birth. She'd been born twenty-four hours after me, on April 11, 1932.

Yane was the dearest friend I'd ever had. The puppy love of our summer together blossomed into romance. I became her lover, her first lover. For six years we met in Alexandria every weekend. We would spend whole days at the beach. The dunes sheltered our love-making. Over a picnic lunch prepared by Yane's mother we would talk about our dreams for the future, with the crashing of the surf in the background. At night we'd go dancing, like every other young couple.

Yane's parents were fully aware of the nature of our relationship. They knew that I was their daughter's steady boy friend and that I would marry her. They were very nice to me and invited me home for dinner at the boardinghouse which the mother ran. Yane's father was a swimming instructor at the royal palace.

The years went by. Yane and I were both twenty-one and I wanted to marry her. I asked my father for his consent. He'd never met my girl friend from Brittany. She lived in Alexandria; we lived in Cairo.

"Who is she?"

He liked the photo I showed him.

"Who are her parents?"

"They're French."

For a Lebanese-Syrian, that's ample reference.

"Is she Catholic?"

"No, Protestant."

"*What?* Protestant?"

The words fell like an ax. My father grew so angry that he seemed headed for apoplexy. It became hopeless to try to reason with him. I gave in to my father and broke off with Yane.

I learned through the grapevine that, shortly afterward, she married a fellow from Alexandria. I also heard that they'd gone to live in Venezuela.

Eleven years later, in 1964, I was representing Egypt at the Bridge Olympics in New York. I sat down at a table to play the opponents who'd been assigned to me at random. They were a man and a woman representing Venezuela. I recognized the woman as my Breton girl friend from Alexandria, my first love. I don't quite remember if I felt a heart pang or a twinge of regret. But I saw that there was an added affinity between us, one we hadn't known before and which brought us together. Neither of us had played bridge when we'd been keeping company and both of us had become champions since then.

My father almost suffered a nervous breakdown because I wanted to marry a Protestant. Eighteen months later I had to tell him that I was giving up my religion, *his* religion, to marry a Mohammedan. I didn't have the courage to face him and, once again, had recourse to my mother. But the unexpected happened. When my father heard the news he had an attack of diabetes. Nevertheless, three days later the marriage took place. The ceremony had to be held in Faten's home.

I can still see the long faces on the whole family—tense, nervous. Coming out of our villa on the way to Faten's, my father paused and ordered, "From now on, I want everybody to be happy. I'm marrying my son!"

Actually, I was married to Faten's father. By Mohammedan tradition, the bride's father must go up to the muezzin who blesses the union.

It was all pleasant enough. My father-in-law and I were standing, our hands joined and concealed by a handkerchief, while the official, pompously designated a sheik, read the clauses of a contract which had already been ratified by mutual consent.

Once this reading had ended, Faten, who'd just become my wife and who, up to then, had been waiting in her room, made her appearance in the drawing room. Dancing girls swayed in time to the music and we mingled with the roomful of guests.

Faten had already been married, so I escaped the ritual of the bridal chamber, the one that involved showing the guests the bloodstained sheet, proof of the bride's virginity. Our wedding gave rise to no other demonstration than a feast.

That was February 5, 1955.

Faten had a five-year-old daughter by her first marriage. Nadia became my daughter when her father died two years later.

5.

MY KISSES ON THE SCREEN sometimes had terrible consequences.

The first kiss led to marriage; the second one practically cost me my citizenship.

In 1967, I was making a western in Hollywood—*Mackenna's Gold*—and I used to have lunch in the studio canteen every day. And every day producer Ray Stark and director William Wyler used to sit down at the next table. They were getting ready to do *Funny Girl* and had begun casting. Barbra Streisand, who'd created the play on Broadway, would be making her movie debut. They were looking for a co-star.

That wasn't such an easy assignment. The screenplay was built around Barbra. What actor would agree to play her straight man?

Fanny Brice sang, cracked jokes, fascinated the audiences; Nick Arnstein (her shady gambler husband) had to content himself with giving her her cues and looking good in a tuxedo, something that didn't improve matters at all. Apparently it was no cinch to find an actor who could look relaxed in a tuxedo. I just happened to be one of those rare individuals, something that started people in the studio canteen joking: "Why not Omar Sharif?"

You can't understand what made this such a big joke, unless you know that *Funny Girl* is set in a Jewish neighborhood of Brooklyn and that it's about a Jewish boy and a Jewish girl. But that didn't matter—they kept up the "Why not Omar Sharif?" campaign.

One day William Wyler reacted. "Well, *why not* Omar Sharif, anyway?" The question had its impact. Dumfounded, they all looked at him. So he repeated, "Yes, that's an idea. Why not? Think about it," he said, turning to me. "It's not such a bad idea at that."

We thought about it and, after thinking it over, became convinced that the idea was a good one. The producer of *Mackenna's Gold* agreed to speed up the shooting so I could be free sooner, and I signed my contract.

That was in 1967. A few days later Arabs and Israelis were locked in the Six-Day War. All the investments in the production were Jewish. The atmosphere of the studio was pro-Israeli and my co-star was Jewish.

Most of the newspapers backed Israel. And I was an Egyptian. An Egyptian from Nasser's regime, one of the Colonel's fellow citizens.

A wave of panic swept over the set. Barbra's mother declared outright, "My daughter isn't going to work with any Egyptian!" Ray Stark spoke of breaking my contract. Fortunately William Wyler, who was also Jewish, reacted strenuously: "We're in America, the land of freedom, and you're ready to make yourselves guilty of the same things we're against? Not hiring an actor because he's Egyptian is outrageous. If Omar doesn't make the film I don't make it either!"

Undecided up to then, Streisand agreed. The producers assigned me a P.R. man of my own. He was to watch over interviews that I'd do, check any statements I made, rectify any tactlessness, if there was any. I cheerfully consented.

The shooting of *Funny Girl* went ahead normally. No

newspaper or magazine stressed my nationality; none tried
to link my country, my role, and the Six-Day War. Everything went smoothly until the day Barbra and I had to
rehearse a love scene.

A New York newspaper ran a photo of it and the photo
wound up in Cairo. The Egyptian press got hold of the picture and mounted a campaign aimed at revoking my citizenship. I was declared a traitor to my country because I'd
kissed a Jewish girl who'd given a gala to raise funds for Israel. The Cairo press knew nothing about our movie, but
they still declared it pro-Israeli—just to make sure.

I got a phone call from the Associated Press.

"What do you think of those articles in the Egyptian
papers?"

"I don't make a point of asking a girl her nationality, her
occupation, or her religion before kissing her—either on the
screen or off."

AP also asked Barbra the same question.

"You really think the Egyptians are angry?" she asked in
reply. "You should see the letter I got from my aunt Rose."
On the spur of the moment, she'd dreamed up an Aunt Rose
who lived in Egypt.

Everybody played along with it. *Funny Girl* came out. I
was very sad. All wars make me sad. I'm anti-nationalist and
I disapprove of religious fanaticism. I hate racism. I hate
anything that could lead one group of people to have contempt for another group of people.

The Six-Day War concerned me personally. I've got blood
in my veins and that blood had something to do with the
feelings that beset me. Yet I knew—I was convinced of it—
that someone, something would stop the Israeli-Arab
conflict. I tried to reason logically, dispassionately.

The racial question—what a good excuse! It's never raised

in vain. Race? It's something we can see. We're born white, we're born yellow, we're born red. They drum color into our heads. And as if that weren't enough, they brainwash us with ideas about good and evil, ideas about wealth and poverty and what not. And, on top of family, class, and race, they add religion! I'm not talking about religious feeling or belief in God. I'm talking about what the various churches do to our feelings and beliefs.

I used to live in an Islamic world, and in catechism class they taught me that, without baptism, I would have kept the stigma of original sin! In that case, were my Mohammedan pals still tainted by the sin of Adam? The priest affirmed this with such authority and conviction that I came close to believing him.

It's the same with nationalism that brainwashes people with a scrap of cloth called a *flag*, with the infantile words of a childish anthem. Doesn't false patriotism creep into sports in the United States? I've never managed to go to a baseball game without hearing the national anthem played to remind everyone that America is the best country in the world. As if the United States wasn't a big enough country to forgo such nonsense! As if it made sense to give millions of people the idea that they enjoy some immense privilege simply by virtue of being born American!

How do we overcome this religious, patriotic, and racist conditioning? How? By love. By loving people. If we just tried to love one another a little, really . . .

As to carnal love, they've never found a substitute for it. Not that I place primordial importance on it. Not that it occupies such a big part in my life. No. For me, making love is something besides momentary pleasure. Don't get me wrong —it isn't something I could forgo. I'm not trying to pass myself off as asexual. But there's lots more to sex than mere gratification. It's never an end in itself.

In view of my reputation for being a lady-killer, this may come as a surprise. But I say, "Down with legends!" I can't understand why some men have to make conquests, unless it's a false virility or a lack of affection.

At the risk of being more candid than I'm given credit for, I'll say that the sex lives of my fellow men are completely shaped by the Oedipus complex. What man has never felt the need (or the desire) to cry on a woman's shoulder? What is the ultimate goal of the lady-killer, if not to find solace in a woman's arms? What have I been looking for? I have never been able to stick to the same woman for long! And yet each of those women has awakened in me love that was deep and sincere (perhaps even purified by physical love).

Making love? It's communion with a woman. The bed is the holy table. There I find passion—and purification. For me, one love drives away another and the woman who's inspiring that love at the time fills my entire world. She's never an object. Unless, perhaps, a sacred object that I put up on a pedestal.

If you believe what reporters make up about me on the basis of remarks taken out of context (but that's the name of the newspaper game, I suppose), I give the impression of making pat statements on the female world. Based on those articles, people could get the idea that I have contempt for the weaker sex. The truth is, I worship women . . . but a certain type of woman. The kind who can use both her intelligence and her femininity. A woman mustn't contradict me openly. She must prove to me, by some means which I prefer not to know, that I'm wrong, and make me change my mind. For instance, by saying to me, "You're right, dear, but don't you think that . . ." Confronting me head on, a woman gives me the impression that she's emasculating me.

On the other hand—and I don't think this can be written off as Middle Eastern atavism—I can contradict a woman because I'm a man and because arrogance is in the nature of men.

I don't understand militant feminism of the women's lib type at all, although I can see its historical justification. It's altogether likely that, if there were no women's lib, a good many changes, rational ones, would never be made. But I'm talking about my own life, my relationships with women, outside the general context, and in this respect I don't give a damn about the world. I'm only concerned with the circles that I move in and, in this limited sphere, I meet women I like. I try to get to know them and to go to bed with them. After tearing myself down, I must admit there's also a positive side to my maleness—I always succeed in having my way. And I make women happy, with the tenderness, love, and thrills I give them. The fact that I'm a movie star, my looks, my prestige—none of that counts. I'm going to be blunt: I get any woman I want because I give all of myself. And who can refuse so much human warmth? Giving, consoling, protecting, guiding—these are a man's privileges. Take them away and you take away his male prerogatives.

The woman, for her part, must give the impression that she needs the man . . . even if she's perfectly capable of running her own life. That's when a woman shows intelligence and femininity.

In this regard, there's one more thing I want to set straight with my fans. People would have them believe that Omar Sharif, the modern seducer, considers women inferior beings. That's untrue. I know from experience that a woman's intellectual level is often higher than her mate's.

More than half of the world's learning comes to us from women. Having said this, I can't go along with the idea of a girl using her gray matter to compete with men. I'd say that she isn't being femininely intelligent.

That's one charge I can't level against Barbra Streisand.

Actually, while *Funny Girl* makes me remember an unfortunate political situation, it's also connected to a wonderful love story.

Barbra Streisand, who struck me as being ugly at first, gradually cast her spell over me. I fell madly in love with her talent and her personality. The feeling was mutual for four months—the time it took to shoot the picture. How many of my affairs seemed to last till the end of a shooting!

Barbra's villa served as our trysting place. At the time, my own villa housed my family. We spent our evenings, our weekends at her place. Our contracts ruled out any travel. The lives of movie stars—at any rate, their movements—are limited by the restrictions imposed by insurance companies that won't accept responsibilities other than those actually involved in making a film.

So, inside those Hollywood confines (about which aspiring young actors dream so much), we led the very simple life of people in love. Nobody could be more conventional, more discreet than a pair of lovers. That's something for prudes to think about.

We used to cook. When I'd used up all my Italian recipes —notably, ones for various pasta dishes which I can cook and season quite well—Barbra would heat TV dinners. I adore Italian food but only eat spaghetti in Italy or when I've cooked it myself. If I get the urge to order spaghetti anywhere else, I go back into the kitchen to supervise the operation. You see, pasta needs lots of room to swim around

in a big pot full of water. That way, it doesn't all stick together. Any kind of pasta has to be tasted every few minutes
so you can tell when it's been cooked enough. Sixty seconds
too long and it's not fit to be eaten. I can't swear to it, but
Sophia Loren's fine Italian cooking must have spoiled me.

So Barbra and I would enjoy simple food; then, relaxed in
our armchairs, we'd watch television. We seldom went anywhere for supper. The first time, I recall, was at Gregory
Peck's place. Greg and I had become friends in the course of
making two pictures together. His wife, a Frenchwoman for
whom I felt great affinity, had strengthened these bonds. I
still see them both whenever I stop in Hollywood.

Like everyone else, Greg knew nothing about the affair
Barbra and I were having, and he had invited me over. So I
asked him if I could bring somebody with me. I knew he
wouldn't let the news out. But if even one reporter happened to be there, that could have ended a romance which
had been delightful (for me, at least)—and all too short.

The years have gone by and I say to myself that Fanny
Brice loved the hero of the movie, that she didn't love Omar
Sharif, that I loved the heroine . . . that I didn't love Barbra
Streisand. It often happens that way. Isn't fiction more fascinating than reality? How pleasant, how easy it is to fall in
love with my female co-stars: I've had so many of these
ephemeral romances. Whenever I make a movie I become
one with the character I'm portraying. Which amounts to
saying that it's hard to stop loving the minute the director
says, "Cut." It's hard to play love scenes all day and then
drop into apathy at night. My co-star is beautiful, they ask
me to love her for weeks, for months—and I'm supposed to
change my feelings as I get back into my street clothes.
Well, I can't always do it. You see, I'm in love because I'm
available and sentimental. Because I'm in love with love.

But have I really loved? I don't know, since I've never suffered from love. They say I'm pathologically unfaithful. No. I'm never unfaithful. I simply fall in love a lot, often and fast.

Did I love my wife? Yes, in the Middle Eastern way. My marriage wasn't a marriage of love, in the sense of passionate love. It was a marriage of compatibility, affection, friendship.

A marriage can thrive on these feelings, for we'd been married ten years and during those ten years I'd never deceived my wife.

Had I been happy? I'd been contented. I'd had contentment for ten years. I'd slipped into routines, ones that I lived by. I had to, while waiting for something extraordinary to happen. And I knew that it would happen, but I didn't know when. The marriage was my waiting room, a comfortable waiting room, in a house that welcomed many friends. We went out very little because, each time we did, we felt like mountain lions breaking into a rabbit hutch. Everyone who's appeared in movies or on TV has had this feeling. Some celebrities—mainly, statesmen—attract crowds. Men like Khrushchev, Nasser, De Gaulle, and Kennedy. I never tried to find out whether Kennedy was really a great statesman, but whenever he went anywhere people pushed and shoved to get near him. He simply magnetized people.

The day after his death, the women's eyes were red with tears in Cairo. They'd been crying over the famous man, not the President of the United States. Could those women even find America on the map? Of course not. And yet the leader of that remote country had become a legend for them.

Let's return to Cairo. My acting career enabled me to satisfy the thirst for love and admiration that we each carry within us. Unconsciously, I had renounced the life of a John Average. My marriage to a movie idol was in keeping with my vocation. It put me on stage in front of the largest possible audience and I wanted to pack the whole world into that audience if I could.

I made lots of pictures in Cairo. Five with my wife, one of these films being directed by her ex-husband. They all did well. Every Faten Hamama picture scored a hit. What was so surprising about that? She'd been a star since she was five. As a little girl, she'd been the Shirley Temple of the Near East and with each passing year her fame had grown steadily.

Should I tell you a secret? That bothered me a bit. She eclipsed me. When I did a picture without her, I felt more my own boss.

Faten was very lovely, with a Middle Eastern beauty (that she still has although she's grown rounder). But her mind was even more seductive than her body. Faten's intelligence came from her heart.

Our son Tarek told me an anecdote that illustrates his mother's character very clearly.

Once Tarek wanted a dog—preferably, a miniature puppy. His mother took him to a pet store where she hefted the weight of each animal. Finally she spotted a miserable creature off to one side, a scrawny, ugly mongrel that looked at her intensely. "I'll take that puppy over there," she said to the pet shop owner.

"But, madam," he said in surprise, "not that mutt—he isn't even healthy."

"Maybe so," Faten replied, "but he's got such gentle eyes. He needs us."

Tarek named him Starlight and the pup came home with a veterinarian who had to stay at his side for days to keep

him alive. It worked, because Starlight came to join me in
Hollywood with the family.

So I hadn't made an international name for myself in
Cairo. I was eclipsed, as I've already said, by my wife's
glory. At times we would work separately. We made low-
budget, corny pictures that gave the people what they
wanted. At the time, the more the audience cried, the
bigger the hit. We also made comedies, with actors who specialized in that type of thing, and musical comedies that
solved the language problem. Because there are many Arab
dialects. Generally the dialects are written in what's called
"newspaper Arabic," more popular than literary Arabic, but
still inaccessible to many.

So I made lots of pictures but I also had the feeling that I
was wasting time—until the day when I was offered the role
of the uncle in *Bonjour Tristesse* by Françoise Sagan. My
wife urged me to accept. I was twenty-four—a young leading man. Putting myself in the role of a middle-aged uncle
didn't excite me particularly, but I went ahead with it. And
the picture turned out to be the success that I needed to get
me rolling again.

Six years went by that way, between the studio, our
house, and friends' houses.

Tarek was five. I thought I'd convinced my wife not to
have another child. My career was just beginning and I
couldn't see myself being burdened with a family. I hadn't
reckoned on Faten's Middle Eastern nature. In the Mideast,
a woman must have a baby to make her marriage real.

When Tarek came into the world I was in Tunisia making
Goha. Two words in a telegram: "Tarek born." The news
delighted me. I had a son. It was my turn to be the happy
Middle Eastern father. For fathers around the Mediter-

ranean basin, having boys is what counts. How would I have reacted to the birth of a girl? I'd rather not think about it.

This son helped me forget the mingled feelings I'd had about making *Bonjour Tristesse*. I'd met the director, Jacques Baratier, when I was shooting the exteriors of *La Châtelaine du Liban*. Baratier was casting a film taken from a book by Adès and Josipovici, *Goha the Simple*, the story of a Tunisian legend. He offered me the leading role, Goha. I turned it down because I didn't think it would go over. It seemed to me that the subject could appeal to only one segment of the public—the Tunisians.

Shortly thereafter I left Beirut for Paris. We were shooting the interiors of *La Châtelaine*. One night I went to the Casino d'Enghien, where I gambled and lost all the money I had with me in France.

As I was about to leave the casino a gentleman, who told me that he was Lebanese, offered me a certain sum. I accepted it, gambled everything—and lost.

The next morning I found a note from the Lebanese gentleman in my box at the hotel desk. He asked me to return the money he'd loaned. I got the balance of my wages from the producer but was still short 350,000 old francs. I phoned Baratier: "If you give me 350,000 francs right away, I'll sign for *Goha*."

That day Jacques Baratier brought me the sum, which was enormous for him. I still wince when I think of what he must have gone through trying to raise the money.

And that's how I wound up in Tunis for eight months—without a franc's worth of salary coming to me.

6.

THAT PERIOD in 1957 marked the first time I'd ever lived outside my country for several months. It was also the first time I'd ever associated with French moviemakers and stars on a regular basis. That was when I met George Schéhadé, a famous Lebanese poet whose works are well known in France. He had written the screenplay for *Goha*.

It was my first contact with the "abstract." I had some vague idea that certain tendencies of art were called abstract but that was the extent of my knowledge. Egyptian art was still in the figurative stage. Surrealism had yet to cross the Mediterranean. Abstract art? Nobody had even heard of it in Egypt.

George Schéhadé's screenplay struck me as beautiful, poetic, but rather hard to understand. It expressed feelings that transcended reason. I felt a bit lost.

The naïve, spiritual Goha falls in love with the wife of the wisest, most respected man in an Arab town. People find out about their affair. According to the law of the Koran, the unfaithful wife must be executed and Goha banished from the community. He must run away. The wise man goes after him, brings him home, gives him food and shelter. He speaks to him about his wife: "She is beautiful, isn't she?" and Goha replies, "Not as beautiful as you, master."

It was a lovely story but it depicted a world where I couldn't set foot. My uncle hadn't introduced me to flights of fancy like this. How could a man be more beautiful than a woman? To my Middle Eastern eyes, this beauty of the mind couldn't be compared to the beauty of a body. No, I'd never learned this kind of thinking; nobody expressed themselves that way. In Egypt, if you went around saying that a woman wasn't as beautiful as a man, you'd be branded a homosexual.

I told George Schéhadé, "I'd like to understand what you've written."

We spent a whole night poring over the script.

"It's very simple," he repeated.

And, as a matter of fact, everything did become clear as day—the odd dialogue, Goha's actions, the wise man's actions, the taut atmosphere, the well-composed shots. Yes, it all came clear in my mind and, with Schéhadé's assistance, I was able to put a lot of human feeling into that Goha.

It was a real event in movie making, one that was ahead of its time perhaps but nevertheless received critical acclaim. And while it didn't enjoy a commercial success in France, the English loved it and have shown the picture on television year after year.

For me, personally, this was an important period in my life, thanks to Baratier and to his assistant, Jean Babilée, who was then at the height of his career. They moved in Parisian intellectual circles, meeting poets, painters, stage designers, and they dragged me along with them. I found it fascinating. I had the feeling that I was discovering both new forms of artistic expression and the people who'd produced them. That reminds me of one of Baratier's observations, as we were beginning to shoot the picture in Tunisia: "You'll see. There's a movie coming out that's going to revolutionize motion pictures." It was *Breathless*. But I'll come back to that later on.

Goha remains a wonderful memory (even if it proved to be the least remunerative picture of my career).

By way of contrast, I want to mention *Dr. Zhivago*. For me, this role was both the most thrilling and the most challenging. Thrilling because I lived the character throughout his lifetime, through my son Tarek, who portrayed the young Zhivago.

David Lean had asked me to direct him. He knew that it was an excellent way of understanding the character. By explaining young Zhivago's actions to my son, I would be getting myself into the mature Zhivago's shoes.

Tarek was seven at the time. He didn't (and still doesn't) resemble me to the point that people could say, "That's Omar Sharif's boy." No, the resemblance isn't physical. He's got my way of thinking, my way of speaking, my way of being, my bearing.

When David spoke to me about Tarek, I agreed—on one condition: no photo of my son would be published. I wanted him to have an ordinary childhood; I refused to make him different from other boys.

Tarek adjusted perfectly to this situation, as new as it was for him. With great facility, he copied the movements and gestures I showed him. In fact, he was so good that offers of contracts came in for him, but I turned them all down.

So *Zhivago* was thrilling because Pasternak's book had been an international best seller. Thrilling because of the director's ability. It was the David Lean of *Bridge on the River Kwai* and *Lawrence of Arabia*. The screenplay had been admirably written. The producer had spared no expense. The direction was precise, the cutting meticulous. There was everything to indicate that the picture would be a hit. And I had the leading role. Why shouldn't I be thrilled?

I'd put in a lot of work, first with the director, then with the scenario writer. I wish I'd been able to meet Pasternak, but he didn't want to leave Russia. I guess he might have had trouble getting back in.

It was thrilling—and frightening, too. Because (and I felt it coming) *Zhivago* left its marks on me. It's the old story. Too big a success can be dangerous for a star. It marks him, it ties him, it limits him. Even today, no matter what I do, I'll always be Dr. Zhivago for moviegoers, and my other pictures, good or bad, will only appear in the background. Let's be fair, I have no regrets—but I sometimes find myself thinking that the ideal screen career involves a succession of modest hits.

A French author once wrote, "Nothing extraordinary is needed for success—at times, being happy is enough." And I've been happy. To repeat, I have no regrets. Yet the actor that I am deep down inside is never entirely satisfied with his performance.

I made a mistake, for a reason that was understandable but unforgivable: I betrayed the scenario writer. Oh, I did it unconsciously, of course, but I did betray him. Dr. Zhivago is an omnipresent character who looks on, watches, feels some emotions, but never expresses anything.

The picture was made in little sections, like all the others. Every day I would shoot different scenes with one actor, then another, and day after day I faced them—actors who acted. I wasn't supposed to do anything but look on, watch, never show a reaction. . . .

I followed those instructions for two months, but the day came when this apparent self-effacement began to disturb me, and gradually I let more emotion creep in than I should have, an inner emotion but one that revealed itself by certain looks or by mime (spontaneous but superfluous).

I let my emotiveness get the upper hand. I couldn't resist the lines that my co-stars spoke. I should have had complete trust in the scenario writer and the director; instead, I let myself fall into the trap. I know that an impassive Zhivago would have been more convincing than Omar Sharif's emotiveness.

And something else happened. During the filming of *Zhivago*, my wife and I separated. We'd been in Spain or Finland, I can't recall any more, when Faten and I decided, by mutual consent, to give ourselves our freedom. This was done slowly, between December 1964 and October 1965. Yes, the eight months that it took to make the picture.

7.

A T THIS POINT I must speak of the long road that
starts at my old home in Cairo and leads to my
solitary life on the Boulevard d'Auteuil in Paris.

As I've already said, my childhood was a sheltered one.
All shocks coming from the outside were absorbed by my
parents' tenderness.

I was six when my sister came into the world. Her health
was delicate. Two or three times everyone thought she was
going to die. She got most of my father's love. He spoiled
her and she became impossible. He wouldn't allow anyone
to scold her. She grew up under my father's total protection,
which entitled her to have her way in everything. If I
wanted to listen to music she'd turn off the radio; she
bothered me, she never stopped bothering me. We fought
constantly.

I was closer to my mother, while my sister formed a bloc
with my father. He was a devout Catholic, so my sister became fanatically religious—for her, everything was a mortal
sin. She disapproved of my conduct, on the outside and at
home, because she felt it wasn't in keeping with her religious ethics.

When I renounced Catholicism to marry a Mohammedan
we came closer to disaster. I'd never been attracted by spir-

itual things. I'd never believed that God created the earth and that He ruled it. My sister's puritanism made it easier for me to hold these views. She certainly contributed to making me into an "awful" atheist. Actually, I love her very much. I love her because she's my sister and because family ties are precious to me. But there was never any alliance between us.

I recall one night when, like so many others, I went dancing with some friends at the Semiramis, a palatial hotel that stood across the street from our house.

At 3:00 A.M., when the waiter brought me the check, I saw that I didn't have any money in my wallet.

"Got some money?" I asked my neighbor.

"No."

"How about you?"

"Me either."

My pals were as broke as I was. An idea dawned on me: "Wait here. I'll be back in ten minutes."

It was out of the question to wake my parents at that hour of the night but I knew that my sister, like a provident bee, kept all her money in a pear-shaped piggy bank.

I went across the street and my first impulse was to ask her for a loan. No, she'd never agree. So I took off my shoes and crept into her room. I grabbed the piggy bank, which was heavy with the coins and bills she'd saved.

Then I smashed the bank and went back to my friends, where I ordered another round of whiskey and generously paid for everything.

The next morning my sister began crying and screaming that I had stolen her piggy bank. I was still sleeping when she "reported the theft."

I understood her reaction, but I was angry with her for telling my father before talking things over with me. I would have paid her back anyway. My father did it for me, but this lack of complicity always bothered me.

At the time, everything seemed to be taking me away from the family atmosphere—my English education, the theater, my uncle, my pals at whose houses in the country I spent weekends.

A bunch of us fellows would go away together. In the Middle East, girls grow up separately from boys. Girls never took part in our games. I was sixteen and girls still weren't admitted to male society. Sometimes on a Saturday we'd get together at what we called "parties," in the presence of a duenna who made sure that the evening was spent chastely.

As for *women*, in the technical sense of the word, we could only admire them at the opera or in the French road companies that played Cairo. Or else we went looking for women in night clubs or on streets set aside for that purpose.

My first sexual relations (as doctors say) were with a prostitute. With a few buddies, I went looking for adventure in Heliopolis, a city close to Cairo.

Sultan Selim once defeated the Mamelukes in Heliopolis, and General Kléber routed a Turkish army there, but my only accomplishment in that town was to take one fallen woman by storm in a sordid alley. The preliminaries were the same as any place: "How much?" Once the price had been set, she had me drive out to a place in the desert near the airport where an enterprising fellow had set up a Coca-Cola stand. In exchange for buying one or two bottles of soda (which cost next to nothing) you were entitled to "parking" under his protection. The Egypt of Farouk wasn't especially prudish, but it didn't tolerate public love-making in parked cars.

On any dark night you could make out fifty or sixty cars—maybe more—each of which housed one or two couples. I was alone with my whore in my first car—something that, in Europe or America, would have established my age quite accurately. But in my country, at that time, no law could withstand money. A driver's license, legally issued at eighteen, might also be had at ten—if you paid the price. I got mine, I think, at fifteen or sixteen.

Once I'd purchased the bottles of blackish liquid I was able to park in the assigned space and finally enjoy the pleasures of the flesh. My companion seemed beautiful. I needed to delude myself to make that first act of "love" less prosaic. She seemed so desirable that I can't erase her from my memory. I can still picture her, only now she seems hideous.

At eighteen, I entered the world of work. I wanted to be an actor, while my teachers urged me to go into mathematics. All my friends knew that I had only one ambition—to become an actor. Only my family pretended not to know about it. They had their way at first.

According to tradition, the son goes into the father's business—especially if that business is doing well. And my father wanted me to carry on in his footsteps.

I was counting on my mother to put pressure on him: "Mother, I can't be a businessman. I just don't like it. I'd like to study in London."

"I'll talk it over with your father. You'll see—I'll convince him. But what do you want to study anyway?"

My mother was convinced that my gift for mathematics would carry me into chemistry or physics.

"Theater."

The cat was out of the bag.

"That I can't help you with. Personally, I've got nothing

against actors, but I can't persuade your father to let his son become a wandering minstrel."

When my mother admitted defeat I had to give up. I put on a merchant's shop coat and my father taught me how to recognize different kinds of wood, to estimate the number of board feet in a log. He introduced me to his clients, who were to become mine. He taught me that merchandise bought for ten francs must be sold at eleven. It was simple. But I didn't get any fun out of that business and it just didn't suit my nature. Maybe other people enjoyed it and found it stimulating. Not me. I was just plain uncomfortable.

I had to try to cheat the next guy, because if I didn't cheat him he'd come and cheat me. This game was totally foreign to me. That's when my father, a very religious man, struck me as slightly dishonest, since all business involved cheating. At least it seemed dishonest compared to the ethics I'd learned both in school and at home. He reassured me: "Business profits are legal. . . ." And yet it all seemed immoral. Everything that was going on in my father's office struck me as immoral.

To convince him that I wasn't cut out for the family business, I decided to start selling at a loss. I inverted the factors. What I bought at eleven francs I sold for ten, under the pretext that my customer had a sick wife, an ailing daughter, or a crippled mother-in-law.

My mother protested: "They're tricking you, they're just telling you stories."

I went still further with my business philanthropy—I gave credit only to the poor, the insolvent.

"Rich people don't need your easy payment terms," I told my father, who was panic-stricken at the size of the losses I'd produced.

This comedy went on for two years and finally overcame

paternal resistance. . . . No, on second thought, it must have been Nasser's revolution that drove my father to utter the words I'd been waiting for:

"You want to be an actor? All right, do as you wish."

8.

I RECALL THAT TRANSITION between royalist Egypt and the Egypt of Nasser. It came overnight, without bloodshed. At dawn—it must have been 6:00 A.M.—tanks came rumbling through the city streets. . . . The revolution was over.

The people had gathered at the waterfront to accompany Farouk to his yacht. I recall that the vessel's name was the *Maroussa*. There was a twenty-one-gun salute in honor of his leaving.

The fabulously wealthy sovereign, who had accumulated a fortune at his people's expense, made off with his treasure, and the people seemed to think that it was perfectly all right. It strikes me that they found it reassuring to see the republicans, who'd been portrayed as cutthroats, acting like gentlemen.

The feudal monarchy made way for the military revolutionaries without a shot being fired, without retribution of any kind.

King Farouk is dead! Long live Naguib!

The name of Naguib stood out, although it wasn't the name of the true leader of the revolution—Nasser.

At the time Nasser was a young officer known only for his leftist leanings. He needed someone to cover the real direction of the turn from royalist Egypt. Among his companions was a distinguished-looking gentleman, graying at the temples, with a serene face and a charming smile, who never had taken a stand against Nasser's revolutionary movement. His name was Naguib. He was just right for reassuring the people. So it turned out to be Naguib who announced the advent of a revolution he hadn't made. He introduced himself as head of the military junta, and the people acknowledged him, the whole world recognized him, and Naguib became very popular even though, as I've said twice, he hadn't played any role in Nasser's revolution.

Overnight there was a new way of life. My mother's card games disappeared from my daily life. The people gave the impression of a psychological well-being and something they'd never felt before—they had hope. The people who lived in unhealthy alleys began to wake up and demand their rights, now that they'd been encouraged to do so.

The elite gradually lost their brilliance and sank into the shadows of oblivion. My father's business, like that of his competitors, took a beating. The landowners watched the shrinking of the railway tracks that crossed their property; agrarian reform had given the serfs all or part of the manorial lands.

It must be pointed out that this land reform didn't do much good for the country's prosperity. Harvests decreased as business went under. Nationalization, followed by the distribution of hundred-square-yard parcels of land to each small farmer, permitted only manual methods of farming; there was no other fertilizer than that produced by each farmer's livestock.

Agrarian reform proved a flop (as it has everywhere) but the rich people became a lot less rich. Which is only fair.

You did get the impression that there had been real progress in the people's living conditions, and you did feel the stirrings of a hope that the centuries had failed to fulfill.

The Egypt of Farouk had been essentially agrarian. It produced cotton and the plantation owners got rich while the cotton-field hands starved. Under Farouk, Egypt had no industry, so there was no working class. With Nasser came the advent of the industrial age, which gave rise to a now sizable working class. If you add to that free education, the creation of schools and hospitals, you get an idea of the new image Egypt had under Nasser.

Most people ignore the fact that bilharzia, a parasite found in rivers, had wreaked such havoc in Egypt that the average life expectancy was just thirty years. All the peasants on the banks of the Nile contracted bilharziasis and died—for want of doctors and hospitals.

Politically, Nasser distinguished himself on both the domestic and foreign scenes. He moved all the pawns on the chessboard of the Middle East. He became their leader by making the first important revolution in the Arab world. Within Egypt, his achievements weren't as significant. With great skill, he accommodated two equally hard-line factions —one pro-Communist, the other pro-American. Not only was he able to get along with both factions, but he exploited them as well. The pro-Communist clique enabled him to flirt advantageously with the Russians, while the pro-American group got him some favor with the West. When Nasser died there was great danger that the reins of government might fall into the hands of one faction or the other.

Sadat, politically colorless, was the ideal successor. But would he be able to meet the challenge? Yes, and with great adroitness. By neutralizing those who favored the Soviet Union and those who favored the United States; by establishing himself with his own people (and the world) in a spectacular move: his reconciliation with Faisal of Saudi Arabia.

In so doing, he made an implicit pact with the oil-producing countries, a pact that has been significant for Egypt's economic and military development.

Sadat went even further. He attempted an opening with the Israelis by agreeing to sit down at the same table with them at "Kilometer 101."

Did he have the backing of his people? It's hard to gauge in advance the reactions of a people little schooled in public affairs and even less in questions of territorial claims.

The Egyptians had always been dominated, colonized. Is it necessary to recall the coming of the Nubians, who put an end to the hegemony of the Pharaohs? Or the incursions of the Phoenicians, Alexander the Great, the Greeks, the Romans, the Turks, France and, finally, England?

My countrymen have always been under the yoke of some other power and have never actually fought for their independence or their freedom. The Egyptian people have no martial tradition and yet they're expected to go to war, just like that, at the drop of a hat, to add a few miles to their territory!

Nasser understood the futility of such an undertaking. To rally the masses, to make them fanatic, he dreamed up the holy war. I've never taken sides on the question of this conflict, but I'm liberal and I know that the existence of the state of Israel can no longer be jeopardized. And why not help the Palestinians set themselves up as a nation? What are the wealthy oil-producing countries doing with their money? They all use Palestinian labor. Couldn't those courageous arms serve their own cause for once?

It isn't a question of politics. I'm not interested in politics. People interest me, their problems interest me. And I know that the liberal Egypt of President Nasser did not succeed fully in its humanitarian mission. Three quarters of the population of Cairo still lives in unwholesome quarters and unemployment has followed the rate of demographic growth.

The privileged have changed sides, the names of the privileged have changed, but they still comprise fifteen hundred to two thousand people, as opposed to thirty-six million poor wretches, three quarters of whom—peasants, workers—shape the destiny of a country threatened by demographic change, a country that acquires seven hundred thousand new mouths to feed each year.

The money that the republicans took from the rich hasn't served to improve the lot of the poor but rather to arm the country. And arms have never helped a poor society to make progress.

Even free education has failed to bring the masses out of their ignorance, because the children of the poor haven't enough time to go to school. They must work in order to live.

A revolution can't be the work of one man, it must be the work of a team. The machinery of the Nasserian state, particularly in the area of economics, was non-existent. The revolutionaries should have forged that machinery without which all plans—even less ambitious ones—are doomed.

And yet the revolution was inevitable. All revolutions are born of injustice and give rise to new injustice.

The revolution in no way changed the methods used in the film industry, which were still geared to two imperatives: speed and economy. To make sure that nothing will ever change, Egyptian movie makers recruit technicians who are imitators, never creators. They see American movies and remake them to fit Egyptian tastes. After ten or fifteen years' experience, they acquire a degree of professionalism but remain imitators. Their equipment has grown old with them. Oh, there's nothing wrong with the stuff, but time and money are still lacking, just as in the old days.

The actors' style hasn't developed either. They're still playing to that same sentimental, emotional audience. As I've emphasized, Anglo-Saxons steered me toward European standards of expression, but my Arab training was beneficial. David Lean's advice became my watchword: "He who does most does least."

Making my first movie in Hollywood, I was astonished by the amount of money, care, time, and brains that went into it. And yet these material or intellectual factors weren't behind my decision to turn down a contract in Egypt when I went back there after *Lawrence of Arabia.*

I couldn't afford to do B pictures that would sell just because my name was on them, pictures that might cut short my career, which promised to be a fine one. Furthermore, there was still that contract binding me to Columbia for seven years. Between two American films, I went back to Cairo, where I stayed for about three months of the year. I would spend those three months, inactive, with my wife, who went on making five Egyptian films every year.

I'd be idle while waiting for an American contract. Then I'd get out my pipe and slippers, but I couldn't really get into the swing of family life because I knew it was just a layover between two trips. I knew I'd be taking off again. I'd got myself caught in the jet-set trap. My wife was out of it.

From 1961 to 1965, until our divorce, Faten and I became good friends and it was as good friends that we broke up.

Generally my American pictures were set in Europe, so I lived abroad. I wasn't at home anywhere.

That was when I felt the need to be with my relatives.

My sister became a mother. In 1959 she'd met a Spaniard

in Cairo and, after their marriage, followed him to his country. She'd grown up—that is, she was pretty, svelte, elegant, with long auburn hair that got plenty of admiring looks. But our personalities still clashed. She is frugal, I spend; she reasons things out, I act on impulse. She has become more religious, I've grown more convinced in my atheism.

The family resemblance people ascribe to us is mere sham. She resembles more and more my father's side; with each passing day I become more like Mother's side.

It's hard for my parents to be so far from their children. I'd like them closer to me.

In 1965, I set up my family in Madrid. There my father opened a timber business—he was happy. And so was my mother, who no doubt found a new gambling set.

Nadia and Tarek were at a boarding school in Switzerland. The tuition was very high and these exchanges influenced my movie career—I signed contracts that I would ordinarily have turned down. For several years the procedure was invariable: for six months I'd reject screenplays that didn't quite suit me; on the seventh month a pressing need for money would force me to accept an offer I'd sneered at up to then. . . . Not that these pictures were automatically bad. It's just that actors are always looking for the made-to-order part.

While this factor has sometimes been influential, it isn't the rule that governs my career.

For example, the Sidney Lumet film, *The Appointment*, was an experiment that I made deliberately. I'd really loved *Twelve Angry Men* and *The Fugitive Kind* with Marlon Brando, and the idea of working under Lumet's direction intrigued me. He was different. He made his cast rehearse a film like a stage play—from one end to the other. For two weeks we rehearsed in the studio, then played before the cameras without stopping, just like on the stage.

This took care of my homesickness for the theater . . . but the movie flopped.

This young director, a typical New Yorker with that special New York-Jewish brand of humor, with that New Yorker's keen sense of show business, had come to Europe for the first time. To Rome more exactly, where he was thrown in with Antonioni's head cameraman and Fellini's head scenery designer. He opened new eyes on old Europe, which was giving him the best that it had. These disciples of the two great Italians, for whom Lumet had tremendous admiration, influenced him so much that American and European styles were juxtaposed, resulting in a hybrid—not Fellini, not Antonioni, and still less Lumet.

But imperfect as this picture was, it remains very important for me. It enabled me to meet what I consider the world's most extraordinary woman: Anouk Aimée, my co-star.

She was, without the slightest doubt, a fine girl who had qualities that I'd never suspected in a woman. Anouk knows exactly how to act with the man she loves. She knows how to please him, she knows all the things her man likes and wants, at the precise moment when he likes them or wants them. She can make him happy by giving him the impression that she's happy too.

Anouk drew her happiness from mine—or, at least she did everything to make me think so. Here's a for instance: once, after a long day's shooting, I really felt like doing what she felt like doing. I wanted to devote that evening entirely to her. I asked her what she'd like.

"*Voilà!*" she replied. "I'm going to tell you straight out what I'd enjoy doing. I'd like to watch you play bridge."

"No!" I protested. "You're kidding."

But she convinced me that she wasn't. She knew, she felt that I had a tremendous urge to play. We went to the club. I played until 4:00 A.M. When I'm around a card table I concentrate so hard that I forget everybody around me. I didn't say a word to Anouk. She sat behind me with a serene, happy expression, although she didn't understand anything about the game.

Anouk was the ideal companion. There was a time when I thought we could make our lives together, but then destiny separated us.

How did it happen? Was it my fault? Or hers? I don't know any more. Yet, at a certain point in our affair, I'd really wanted to marry her, but the need to safeguard my independence must have won out . . . and experience proved that I was right.

There we were, a few years afterward, two old pals bumping into each other at the Fox studios in Hollywood. Anouk was in love with Albert Finney, who became her husband; I was thinking about another woman for whom I wouldn't have yielded an iota of my freedom.

Anouk was making Lawrence Durrell's *Justine* for George Cukor. I was Che Guevara on the set next door.

One day Zanuck, Cukor's producer, called me: "I've got a dramatic problem to solve. Anouk Aimée wants to drop the picture—she can't stand being away from her lover. If she does that she won't be working any more—ever. She'll have a big fat lawsuit on her hands and she'll be all washed up as a movie star. I know you two are still very close, so please try to reason with her."

I agreed to do what I could to convince her that she was making a mistake. In vain. But at least she consented to phone Albert Finney, who encouraged her to finish the picture.

9.

A NOUK AIMÉE ALSO GAVE ME JOY—the joy of meeting Fellini. That was in May 1967. As usual, he was getting a film ready. I don't remember which one it was, but he was looking for a leading man. Fellini was always after a character. Like a hunter, he stalked the person who would be his star.

I'd seen all his movies. I hadn't liked them all, but I said to myself, "This guy is a great director!" I could feel the stamp of greatness on his work. While he hadn't satisfied me as a spectator, he had impressed me as an actor. For me, Fellini ranks as the greatest director of all time.

Several times in Rome, he invited Anouk and me to dinner at his home. The man captivated me. Every time I listened to him speak I could feel his work taking shape. I understood its mechanism. I saw how he did what he did, because he was what he was.

Fellini sees things nobody else sees. He knows how to look, but most of all what makes him different is the scope of his gaze. Everyone focuses his attention on that aspect of things most specially suited to his own nature. Fellini sees only what is essential. Right away.

For instance, he doesn't miss the woman selling strawberries in the street. She embodies life for him. But it isn't because he connects her with movies that he sees her; it's because movies are within him that he sees the strawberry vendor and that he puts her in his films.

Likewise for prostitutes: he knows how to see them, he loves them. They interest him and he shows it. I love whores too. They have an extraordinary way of making their living by selling their bodies as other people sell vegetables or peanuts. The idea of being able to "rent" an extremely intimate part of myself without giving anything of myself fascinates me.

I'm making a mistake saying that whores sell their bodies; actually they only lend them, and that's not easy. We all lend our bodies every day in one way or another. When I make movies I lend my body, my face, I lend everything except that intimate part bartered by whores and that's what I find so fascinating about them.

I didn't interest Fellini, I didn't inspire him. I'm the product of an artificial society. Fellini likes people in the rough. I've got to admit that I'm not a Fellinian actor.

My actor's nature carries me toward the big spectacle. For me, the best films are those taken from very good novels, written by very good writers. I am Omar Sharif, I don't feel like playing Omar Sharif. I'm "a body for rent," as Louis Jouvet used to say. My thrill comes in disguising myself, hiding myself under a costume, under a name that isn't mine. What a thrill being somebody else for a few days or weeks! Not for the sake of being somebody else, but for being able to play on the feelings of millions of people, being able to make them dream, letting them—like myself— get away from themselves.

That gives you some idea of how far I am from author-dominated films. I don't like having an author impose his will. I accept the fact that he demands veracity for his characters. I believe in the dialogue, but not in scenes like this:

"React the way the director wants."

"But I have the feeling that the hero should act like this."

"You'll see I'm right when we start editing," says the author.

Once the picture has been edited, it often turns out (but it's too late by then) that the actor's instinct was right.

Even if the actor isn't too bright, he's generally got an instinct that doesn't make mistakes. He knows what he's giving to the audience, he feels what he must make them understand. And it's this instinct that tends to trip up the author-director.

It is said that the author-dominated film doesn't lend itself to well-known faces the audience identifies with other roles. It is also said that the authenticity of a social or human condition must come through the anonymity of the heroes, since they are supposed to represent John or Jane Doe.

Actually, the author-director is a superactor. He plays all parts through the intermediary of living puppets (I use this word without any pejorative connotations).

At any rate, a revolution, one born in France, came with the *nouvelle vague*. Jean-Luc Godard was to influence all young film makers—especially, in America, with his *Breathless*. With a free and easy sureness, Godard gave the story its very personal meaning, in contemporary language, scoffing at the strict rules demanded by the cinema. Eliminating overly artificial, overly perfect lighting, knocking over the established rules of editing, he created a new cinematographic writing. But he was counting on his actors.

Breathless didn't just make Godard a big name—it marked the start of a great acting career: Jean-Paul Belmondo's. And everyone knows that Belmondo was instrumental in the success of the movie.

Lined up behind Godard are those who claim to be his

disciples. For a while the *cinéma engagé* replaced "conventional films" and the motion picture industry found itself at a dead end. It was dishonorable to make commercial movies, especially in France, where for a film to be in a bad light "intellectually" was considered an inherent defect.

The critics played a major role in this crisis. Unconsciously perhaps, but that made it easy for them to torpedo superproductions. With a few exceptions, the critics boycotted expensive pictures and worshiped low-budget productions. Why? Let's say that, from the moment substantial amounts of money are involved, the director's work seems less meritorious to them. Actually, it's no easier or harder to handle a scene involving a large cast than it is to direct two characters who can hold an audience. It's neither easier nor harder to direct an expensive movie than a shoestring production.

Both Fellini (to whom I would give top honors among author-directors) and Buñuel have had recourse to actors. So the use of "puppets" doesn't strike me as being absolutely necessary in author-director films. At any rate, the author-directors, even the ones who've proven their mettle, haven't replaced the traditional directors—the kind I'd call story-tellers.

In this category, I put David Lean at the top of the list. Not because we've worked together but because his career is studded with smash hits: *Brief Encounter, The Bridge on the River Kwai, Lawrence of Arabia, Doctor Zhivago*, none of which are to be sneezed at. Not by a long shot. Even today, he's the only director to whom Hollywood gives carte blanche, with regard to both the selection of his subject and his budget.

Having said this, I won't dispute the need for the motion picture "revolution." But I can't stand a director appealing only to my mind—that strikes me as pretentious. Ideally, mo-

tion pictures should reach the mind through the heart. Long
live shows that are aimed at everyone! Long live Charlie
Chaplin, who appeals to kids and intellectuals! But the advent of audiovisual communication abruptly set the bounda-
ries of motion pictures. Long unknown, reality entered the
home via television. Barely twenty years ago it was possible
(even in France) to reach old age without ever seeing pictures of starving children or men mangled by cannon fire.
Only motion pictures showed all.

Which explains the success of war movies. It was something people had never seen. Now people don't have to pay
to see such films. Each night they get their ration of cruelty,
violence, and fighting.

Italian neo-realism has seen its day for the same reasons.
The public grew tired of seeing its own misfortunes on the
screen. They like a good cry at the movies but, preferably,
over somebody else's misfortune. Crying over the loss of a
loved one is real suffering; crying over the death of a movie
hero is something quite different. It's a moment of emotion
that verges on pleasure. You're not personally involved.

One other thing: the days when a face and a name
sufficed to draw, move, or entertain the public may be over.
The star is going to die out. Why not?

In 1968 motion pictures changed in the United States.
That year marked the end of the great Hollywood that
hadn't been able to keep up with the times, that wasn't in
touch with its audience.

Even back in 1953, at the end of the Korean conflict,
young people had shown their disapproval of the nation's
passive attitude to the war on the mainland of Asia, a war
which seemed senseless to those youngsters. The boys who'd
been drafted into the army during the Korean conflict had

experienced the disparity between two worlds: one golden, the other miserable.

Television would become the ally of those young people, who had begun to open their eyes on a world of starvation and oppression. And then came the Vietnam War, and this window on the horrors of all war opened still wider and the number of angry young men grew larger. Their rebellion reached a whole generation, one that refused to applaud *Mutiny on the Bounty,* or Liz Taylor in the diamond-studded trappings of *Cleopatra,* or the other Hollywood extravaganzas. The world—their world—was in flames.

These gigantic frescoes, along with others that cost equally outrageous sums (ranging from forty to fifty million dollars), flopped. The public just wouldn't go along with them any more. The money invested was never recovered.

America was discovering the underground cinema.

Some young film makers who had joined the "new wave" wanted to express themselves. They showed their films in Hollywood where the greats of the motion picture world, who had no desire to move aside for these "young pups," held them in check.

Then the unions stepped in, powerful as they were, closing the doors of the studios to these young film makers who threatened their livelihood. It wasn't a confrontation of two generations so much as a conflict between the "haves" and those who just wanted to have.

These new film makers went out, camera in hand, wallets thin, and brought back films in keeping with the aspirations of youth: peace of mind, peace of body, independent thinking, rejection of a mercenary society. And the films made in the streets showed America its own face, one it had never seen because it had refused to look.

Censorship, which had been strict, became more relaxed, and this was an important factor. The new cinema gradually

With Terence Young. REPORTERS ASSOCIÉS

The Night of the Generals *with Philippe Noiret.*

With Catherine Deneuve during the filming of Mayerling.

Che!

In The Horsemen.

took root in Hollywood. Some of these underground films reached the public and became "commercial." They pumped fresh blood into the motion picture industry of the United States.

At the same time an actor created a new style. He was Marlon Brando. He changed not only acting technique but also the behavior and habits of a generation that adopted the T-shirt and jeans, and I don't think that the influence of Elia Kazan or other teachers from the Actors' Studio had anything to do with this.

Marlon Brando did what no actor had done before. He imposed his style, his expression, and his wardrobe. He was the forerunner of the budding actor films. Brando often met opposition—from both fans and critics—because he was bad sometimes. But these weaknesses enhance his talent. I mean that what characterizes great actors is daring to be bad in the pursuit of the best. Average actors are always average. They never go far enough to risk being bad.

Marlon Brando has no equivalent in the seventh art: he is —all by himself—a school. He injected a new plasticity into movement, gesture, facial expression. This pleasant plasticity, spectacular in the noble sense of the word, although appearing natural, spontaneous, is the fruit of long inner toil. Marlon Brando did away with unnecessary gestures. Austerity is the keynote of his way of moving and looking.

His influence on young actors has been immense; they have all tried to follow his lead. Even James Dean, who thrilled the crowds, was following in his footsteps.

For Marlon Brando, the problem is that he has a political soul, which very nearly cut short his career. It doesn't do to have opinions in the all-powerful motion picture world when you're an actor and nothing but an actor. And then, miraculously, along came *The Godfather* and *Last Tango in Paris,* which put him back in the saddle. Destiny was watching over him. It would have been scandalous if openly stated political opinions had put an end to the "artistic" expression of the greatest actor of our time.

I knew Marlon Brando—No, I didn't really know him. What's more, who can claim to really know him? A few close friends? Not even they! Marlon Brando is being drawn into himself. He doesn't reveal himself. Even approaching him is hard. His inner life—what he loves, what he knows— seems to be enough for him.

I'm better acquainted with Jean-Paul Belmondo. True, I made a picture with him, my first French picture. That was *Le Casse*, directed by Henri Verneuil. Verneuil had an enormous budget available as distributor. *Le Casse* was a French production made in the style of big American productions.

That was 1971. My career had reached the crest of the wave. But Hollywood, meanwhile, had fallen into the trough. Only a foreign extravaganza could rival the budgets of my usual employers, and *Le Casse* was such a production. So that's why I work in France. Because American motion pictures are in trouble.

I met Jean-Paul Belmondo and we discovered a common passion—boxing. On March 8, 1971, we were shooting in Athens. On the same day, in New York, Mohammed Ali put his world's heavyweight title on the line. He and his adversary, Joe Frazier, were evenly matched. It was the fight of the century, but Greek television wouldn't broadcast it.

Jean-Paul and I decided to violate all the rules of prudence imposed on us by contract. We chartered a jet to go to Rome to see the boxing match, which was being shown on Italian TV. It took place at 5:00 A.M. Italian time. At 8:00 A.M. we had to be on the set. It was out of the question to ask for a postponement—not even twenty-four hours. The producer and director must know nothing of our Roman escapade. We took off with our make-up men and wardrobe men. At zero hour we were on the set, ready as the day before, ready as the following day. Nobody ever found out that we'd spent the night in Italy.

You have to love boxing to pull a stunt like that, right? Sure, I do love boxing and, for the same reasons, I think, as Jean-Paul Belmondo, although I've never actually been in the ring. Boxing is a man's sport, a brutal sport practiced in a brutal atmosphere. The spectacle is both in the ring and at ringside. Sitting among prize fight fans is a delight.

As for *Le Casse*, it appeared in my life line as my astrologer had described it three years before: "In 1971 things will begin improving," and . . . I'll tell about that in a little while.

In fact, while my motion picture success brought me lots of money, my investments had gotten me into financial difficulty.

Le Casse was the first film that I had a share in. Aside from my salary, I got a commission on the receipts, and the film did well at the box office. What a pleasure! I made money and had fun making the picture.

I grew up with Greek kids in Alexandria; it was a thrill for me to live in their ancestral land. I loved their music, their songs, their food.

I played the part of an unlicensed policeman, something which didn't exactly fit my experience but was so different that I got into the role enthusiastically. Something that hadn't happened to me in six years . . . since *Zhivago*.

Verneuil is a "conventional" director. I mean that he's trying to tell a story, and it's very pleasant for an actor to tell a story in gestures. What's more, Verneuil is a Middle Easterner. Actually, his Armenian blood makes him more oriental than I. We got on well right from the start.

There was Jean-Paul Belmondo, charming, easygoing. There was Robert Hossein, Russian, very oriental, senti-

mental, highly melodramatic, with an extreme sensitivity
that he knows how to express.

We had plans for doing a play together. He was to direct,
I would act. We even decided which play we'd do—one that
takes place in South America. We got together several times,
we talked about it for hours, and the plan fell through. The
playwright refused to let us put it on. Out of professional
scruples. He just didn't like it any more. And that's often the
way it goes in show business.

My "movie destiny" had—I must confess—nearly been
sealed in Paris, back in 1963. Fred Zinnemann was shooting
the exteriors of *Behold a Pale Horse*, a picture that I did
with Gregory Peck and Anthony Quinn.

I was a good Spanish priest in an anti-Fascist story that
brings patriotic feeling roused by the war into conflict with
filial and maternal love.

Alexandre Trauner, teammate of Marcel Carné, Billy
Wilder, Orson Welles, and so many other greats, did the
sets. We became friends.

"I'd like you to meet Jacques Prévert," he said to me one
day. "He's just written a screenplay with a leading role that
would fit you like a glove."

Trauner told me the plot. I loved it, but the film was
never made.

The story, set in the time of the Renaissance, is taken
from a collection of short stories by a Swiss writer, Gottfried
Keller. A young priest in a small provincial city decides to
convert the girls in the local whorehouse. To do this, he
pays the madam for a trick with each girl, who, little by little, yields to the priest's powers of persuasion or charm. He
goes upstairs with the girls one by one, but only to preach
the gospel. One of the girls, an incorrigible prostitute, is just
as determined to "convert" him. To avoid all physical con-

tact and to preach in comfort, he is obliged to tie her up, but she stubbornly resists his appeals. He refuses to give up, so his money melts like snow in the sun. Finally he is reduced to stealing from the collection box to pay for his expensive preaching, which has become a mere pretext for his sexual impulses. He winds up a murderer.

Jacques Prévert—through the films of Marcel Carné—had been the poet of my adolescence. His film dialogues enchanted me. As I had some deeply rooted preconceptions at the time (part of the cultural heritage from my uncle), I went to Prévert's house convinced that I was going to find a man who looked like Baudelaire. Instead I found myself face to face with a member of a Parisian youth gang. He had lots of common sense and spoke in such simple language that he seemed ordinary. Yet, without my realizing it, every one of his words sank in because, on my way home from that first talk, everything he'd said came back to me and I realized that I had seldom heard words used so well to describe precise situations.

We saw each other many times after that. Prévert talked and I still got the same thrill listening to him. We made up our minds to set up a motion picture company with his brother Pierre and Alexandre Trauner.

For a whole year we got together at regular intervals over bottles of red wine and salami. We would talk and talk about our plans. Before long Prévert wanted to bring in a friend, then another, none of whom knew anything about motion pictures and each of whom needed a job. I had my feet on the ground—thanks to my sojourns in Hollywood— and knew that making a movie was no philanthropic endeavor. And I was in no position to be a patron of the arts. Our film company never got off the ground, but Prévert has remained an excellent friend. He enabled me to meet other people, people who didn't belong to the acting world. Knowing Jacques Prévert was a lucky break.

So was meeting Samuel Beckett. That privilege was given to me in 1966. I had a friend, an Irishman like him, Jack MacGowran, who died in 1972. He belonged to the circle of Beckett's close friends and was his favorite actor. Jack often came to Paris to see him. For me, each of his trips was the occasion for a pleasant evening. Once he told me, "I'm going to introduce you to a wonderful man."

That wonderful man was Samuel Beckett. His *Waiting for Godot* was, to me, the most exciting play written by a contemporary author. I'd seen it and been thrilled.

Samuel Beckett. I had put him in the same category as Shakespeare—which gives you an idea of how I felt about him.

So one evening I went to the Montparnasse restaurant, Aux Îles Marquises, to which we'd been invited. I had the feeling that I was going to meet Melpomene and Thalia, brought together for my pleasure. I wasn't disappointed. He made a great impression on me—with his physical beauty, his intellectual nature, the precision of his thinking.

I understood why he had refused to give interviews and had shied away from all contact with the press: the purity of his thoughts could find no better means of expression than from his own pen. Any outside intervention might have deformed it.

Four times in one month we gathered around the same table in the same restaurant. Beckett is a solemn man, in the way he drinks and eats, in his language, stripped of big words and ready-made expressions. What a lesson! The great artists express themselves simply, whether it's Beckett, Prévert, Fellini, Chaplin, or Norman Mailer, just to mention a few. In plain, direct language, they talk about everyday things. Meanwhile, those who haven't achieved recognition and who still aspire to fame employ highfalutin, complicated, stilted language. Maybe that marks the difference between real talent and the phony. The real one hits the bull's-eye, he gets right to the point. The phony beats around the bush.

Beckett captivated me. He told about a play in progress, one that he was writing with Jack MacGowran in mind. He spoke about Ireland.

Samuel Beckett is Irish. His soul is Irish. And he's deeply in love with France. He speaks French fluently; what's more, he writes in French. And Beckett knows how to listen. He's a wonderful conversationalist.

I'd have liked to act in a Beckett play, but I'm not one of his characters. I don't belong to his world any more than I do to Fellini's. Am I sorry? No. We've got to be what we are, and I'm rather fond of being me. But there's no law against dreaming.

That same year I was "officially" adopted by France, or at least I got that impression. I took part in the "Thursdays" of Georges Pompidou, then Premier.

Each week, on Thursday, at the Hôtel Matignon, a film was shown, followed by a dinner party to which at least eighty people were invited. These guests came from very different circles. You could meet bankers or diplomats, doctors, actors, sculptors, painters . . . you name them. These soirees of the Premier and his wife (who played an important role in them) were held with great simplicity, without protocol. For the space of an evening our hosts were plain folks trying to forget the weighty responsibilities of their office.

The films were shown in a basement, the dinners were
held in the private banquet rooms of the Matignon. A perfect hostess, Madame Pompidou knew how to make everyone feel at home.

Georges Pompidou loved to give commentaries on the
films. He took obvious pleasure in discussing art with the
film makers. I often had the opportunity to talk about
movies with him. He was a competent and enlightened
moviegoer.

Those soirees were pleasant times. That's the correct ad-
jective. And, to my mind, life should be a succession of
pleasant times.

This idea, which makes no claim to being a philosophy of
life, is very dear to me and sums up my general outlook.
There I go again being Middle Eastern.

Middle Easterners are lazy. They don't make plans. I
don't make any. Other people make them for me, and I accept them to the extent that they give me—directly or in-
directly—"pleasant times."

The paradox is that I've often felt like working with great
men, like Beckett and Fellini, but I've never wanted to play
a particular role. I'm frequently asked which character I'd
like to portray. I don't know. I've never given it any
thought. I wait for them to come to me.

So much for life—but what about death? Am I afraid of
death? I don't think about it, but I am superstitious.

It's true that I'm an atheist, but some of the superstitions
of my Catholic childhood still persist in me. So dying is connected with heaven, hell, and purgatory. They taught me
Descartes, so I'm a rationalist. And yet the mention of death
takes me back to childish ideas of good and evil. These no-
tions do have some impact on my thinking, but superstition

—since I consider it as such—doesn't dominate my important decisions. In other words, when I feel like doing something I'm not prevented from doing it. And I rely on my mind for this.

Nevertheless, some little everyday things are connected to my superstitions. For instance: I won't work on a set where somebody is wearing an article of clothing or something that's purple. This color reminds me of Holy Week, when everything is decorated with purple. And purple means death. Pagan superstition or not, it's still in me. So, in any studio where I'm working, purple is forbidden.

I also have my gambler's superstition—green eyes. If I feel them looking down at my cards I become paralyzed. I know they're going to make me lose. And I'm not a masochist—I don't play to lose.

Now take Vittorio De Sica; he used to play for the fun of it. He would never leave a game with a penny in his pocket. As long as he had a chip left or the possibility of credit, he would throw it all on the gambling table with the greatest joy. He lost a hundred fortunes in the casinos. He used up his life working so that he could afford to lose the fruits of a film in one night.

Me, I like gambling, but I also like to win, and green eyes make me lose every time. I've had it happen. Every time a green eye has lighted on my hand, the game ended—at my expense.

Each time that purple clothes have moved around on a set where I was working, spotlights fell from overhead cat-walks, with near-fatal results.

I'm very attached to my superstitions because they have proven to be right. In the same way, I believe in astrology. A horoscope made in 1968 revealed myself to me. The astrologer worked it out with such precision that I thought this was the real me. It describes my character with astonishing thoroughness. The predictions for the next seven years came true—right down to the last detail. I'm compelled to believe in astrology.

10.

[Omar Sharif let me have this horoscope, excerpts from which follow, calling my attention to the fact that he was not consulted. The astrologer worked on the basis of the place, date, and exact hour of his birth.—M.-T.G.]

THE SUBJECT'S SIGN OF THE ZODIAC is Aries with a Libra ascendancy, such that he is a Uranus-Moon type with regard to planetary influence.

"Uranian of Aries, he is a creature of fire. His essential values correspond to energetic, dynamic data, and total expenditure of motricity. A nervous muscular motricity, voluntary or cerebral, but I believe it to be nervous.

"From deep within, he tends to spurt a compressed, dry strength, which is basically explosive and at home in speed, fervor, excitement and paroxysm.

"This person is made to release new forces that forge an abrupt, whole, free, sensation-loving character, given to audacious, if not extremist solutions, possibly inclined to promote, innovate, renew.

"He lets himself be carried away by his own bursts of passion and, when this power is blocked by an inner conflict, which happens frequently, this strength turns into great tension and into nervous agitation.

"I have the feeling that, within this person, there is a kind of intense vital pulsation, on the basis of which he thinks of himself as a being made to be launched like a rocket into space.

"Thus, there is an element of violence in him, an element of recklessness which makes his life an adventure, a permanent risk.

"This subject is a person who has no ancestors, no parents —from the psychological point of view, of course. He has an orphan's complex—that is, he has not been fed on the original life pulp of his parents. He was isolated very early from the parental milieu; in any case, he has experienced a feeling of distance and estrangement with regard to them. Even if his parents were well off, he's not a prodigal son. He seems to be a boy isolated in the family cell.

"He is a child of that life which has no past, because he lives only in the possibilities of what is called the future. All reminiscences of the past are suppressed in him. Thus, for him, it's all a matter of creating or re-creating, not re-creating things with respect to what comes before, but to make himself over constantly. He is constantly on the go.

"He tries to live in a continual tension that wears him out. Thus, he is outside the ordinary climate and what he can't stand is anything that is basically ordinary, established, routine.

"He is the enemy of anything that makes things level, anything that mixes, anything that confuses, anything that tranquilizes or makes secure. He lives at the peak of his possibilities; he is therefore quite demanding of himself. He belongs in the insomniac category because such a temperament prevents one from sleeping. Give him all the success in the world—he's already had success, he has a career, he has a name, he already has many things, but give him all the success in the world and he still won't sleep—he can't. He's a person on the alert who needs to keep going further and still further.

"Bachelard has defined this type of personality as a 'Prometheus Complex.' What did he mean by that? A tendency to go further, even further than his masters, going beyond his masters. Trying to be his own master, going beyond himself.

"The myth of Prometheus involves fire, so we see once again the basic element. The subject is identified, is confused with the original fire.

"He also confuses desire and reality. Why? Because, in him, there is naïveté, gratuitousness, and purity that make of him a creature of the immediate. He is total, whole. His life is all or nothing; it's the absolute.

"His destiny is a big win, but he has a tendency to win big every week. Like Prometheus, he defies the universe. But Prometheus ended in chains because he robbed the celestial fire.

"Everything about him is forced and excessive.

"The dominant trait of his character is independence. He belongs to no one; he scarcely belongs to himself. His refusal of the chains is total. He is a bachelor who can become attached; when he does, he goes all out—but for how long? For the moment, not for tomorrow. He isn't built for living side by side with a woman but, rather, for living in a free union.

"In his astral sky, a conjunction with Venus has a distant bearing on religion. There could be a religious influence on love or the influence of love on religion. Just as there may be a relationship between love and foreign lands, I could easily see a certain degree of emotional exoticism in him.

"He can be interested in women of a type different from his own.

"For him, kissing a woman is to embrace part of the universe, while he has a fierce eye for women. He is horribly cruel and, in certain respects, a sadist. With regard to women, he can be as kind as he is malicious. The two feelings coexist in his way of loving. He's a handsome infidel who can be faithful, since there are ties that can last."

[*This side of Omar Sharif's personality seemed incompatible with his generous nature and his affable, considerate ways. I questioned him on this particular point of his character. I tried to get confirmation—in vain.—M.-T.G.*]

Making my own self-criticism, I'd say that I'm cruel because of my selfishness. I gather everything around me. I am the center of my concerns. When I say that the world and the universe don't interest me, that's just a figure of speech. It's a reflection of my intimate feelings and, implicitly, the confession of a frenzied but involuntary selfishness.

Selfishness leads straight to cruelty, since it makes you close your eyes to the feelings of others who must therefore suffer. I live and see through myself, I'm geared to myself. And that's what happens with women.

As soon as a relationship gets me down, I feel so oppressed that I cease to exist physically, mentally. Overnight, I'm not there any more. I know that this escape is an act of cruelty, but I don't look at it that way. . . . And neither do my partners, since none of them has stood in my way.

I've gone on being friendly—even loving—with every woman who's lived with me. They were all discerning enough to sense that such an attitude formed an integral part of my personality. They all knew that, sooner or later, I would leave them. I am passionate in love, as in everything, and passion lasts only so long. And then, I must admit, the development of an emotional commitment frightens me, makes me anxious, oppresses me. The greater this development, the harder the breakup. Then I just disappear, without apparent reason.

A love affair that's too good prompts me to run away, because I know that sooner or later I'm going to have to run. . . . So I'd rather leave while I have pleasant memories. This is a kind of masochism that collides constantly with my latent egotism.

As for fidelity, I do give it some importance, but not as much as sincerity. I'll explain this. I could allow my wife to have sex with another man but I couldn't accept her deceiving me. To deceive me, she'd have to lie to me. Infidelity is a weakness that can be forgiven; cheating on me is deceit and I hate that. Going home with another man after a drinking party is wrong. But making a date with the same guy is cheating. It's a question of premeditation.

I impose the same rights and the same duties on myself: sin, but never deceive. In emotional and sexual terms, both partners should be perfectly equal . . . although this should reflect each one's needs. I think men feel the need for sex more frequently than women do. For the man, it's also a game that must be played in the company of his pals. Pals are part of the male world. They are an essential component of that world and men, among themselves, are cowardly and vain. Cowardly in the face of mockery; vain in proving their manhood.

[*Let's go back to the astrologer's analysis of the actor.* —M.-T.G.]

"In the background, I see moral and spiritual elements that give him a different image than that of the superficial movie star, living an animal existence without concern for the problems of others. I think that there are still a great many things to be revealed in him.

"There are still untapped resources. His career benefits from a Jupiter current of the highest order and, perhaps, motion pictures seem to suit him best, motion pictures with their artificial side in the artistic sense of the word. The movies offer technical means that make escape possible.

"His freedom is of prime importance but, in the background, I discern a marked over-individuality, as well as a 'psychic inflation.' What do I mean by psychic inflation? The power to mass, to mobilize all his forces on a given point of himself and, if this precise point is his ego, he can then amplify himself. In other words, in movie terms, I think that he is built for playing character roles and not situations. He gives his heroes the totality, the power, the incandescence of his own person. His ability to identify with a character is extremely great.

"Given his inner strength, he had a pressing need to succeed, to make a name for himself, to become a somebody, to leave his mark on this planet; if not, he would have become paranoiac. He would have begun raving about some illusory grandeur.

"His sky is the only one of its kind. It would take a millennium, perhaps a million years, to find that same sky. On the other hand, it is possible that, in Alexandria, on April 10, 1932, at 5:30 P.M., one or two other boys and a few other girls were born. With respect to the stars, these children could be called twins. All of these astrological twins had to break out of their anonymity. Perhaps the others did not achieve his fame, but they have made a name for themselves in their own circles; if not, they must be raving paranoiacs with delusions of grandeur.

"In his own life, he is an adventurer with a love of strong

emotions, intense feelings, and one who, when he gambles, has the feeling at times that he's gambling with his destiny, that he's staking everything. That's part of his world. He's an adventurer in the purest sense of the word.

"If he'd been born in 1820, he would have sailed for America at the age of eighteen, in hopes of making a fortune or playing the conquistador. One can imagine him at different periods in history, but always out in front, setting the example, figuring as an idol.

"He has skin-deep emotions constantly brought into play by events around him. An adolescent completely devoted to the ebb and flow of an impulsive sensibility, he is ruled only by whim and follows his fancy unconstrained, which accounts for his extreme physical mobility. A fluttering, fun-loving butterfly that flits here and there as life takes him, wherever the wind carries him. He lives in the intensity of passing emotions, savoring new sensations. A fugitive soul, vagabond, restless, undisciplined, in search of novelty, style, diversion, temptation. But he is also wood drifting to the whim of the oceans, frail under the eddies of inner waves, at the mercy of fits of emotion or storms of rootlessness, if not actual psychic immaturity. Such are the two personalities that exist in a perpetual dualism within this subject.

"This first personality symbolizes strength, vitality, will, passion. It is driven by an inner current that prompts it to 'do something' and to put all its eggs in one basket to reach the goal which it has set.

"The second lunar personality is characterized by emotivity and intense sensibility; and this inner duality is typical of many artists born under the sign of the Ram.

"For them, the summit is to taste life's fruit, especially the forbidden ones, and to refuse, at all costs, to live an ordinary life.

"I have also called attention to one element—psychic mobility which drives him toward change, variety, the need to see new scenery, new faces, complete changes of setting.

"The first personality—headstrong, disciplined, stern—weds that which will bring him the greatest intensity, but he has a Draconian severity in certain regards. Meanwhile, the second personality is whimsical, a gambler, with a taste for things that are free, poetry and cynicism.

"He shows his cards easily and quickly. The moment he expresses his emotion, he no longer feels it. If he were to create himself, it would be out of playlets, well-turned poems, moments of music.

"To define his personality: two components—the Uranian and the Lunar—coexist within him.

"The Uranian is ultravirile, hypermale. The second character is feminine, but it has a soul and that means identification with the values of the female psyche. He is very close to the world of women. Within him is this coexistence, one that can produce odd things. I am carrying this to an extreme, but this individual is an extreme."

[*Omar also gives an explanation about this dual "membership." He does so without trickery.—M.-T.G.*]

The male who "lays" a girl can't satisfy her. Love is a complex game. Winning it takes lots of trump cards and a vast knowledge of psychology. I know from experience that a woman is only happy when she's with a man who really understands her. And really understanding the female psyche calls for having a bit of the female in you. I'll go even further. To make a woman happy in bed, you've got to be half man and half woman. The converse is equally true.

The most sensual mistress would be a girl with lesbian tendencies. What's more, I think that lots of women could be lesbians—at any rate, the more sensual ones.

On the other hand, the male doesn't have the same natural predisposition to homosexuality, although I'm aware that history contradicts me. But *you've got to get an erection over a man*, which doesn't make sense. Personally, I couldn't do it. Unlike the Greeks, my aesthetic sense is offended by two male bodies having intercourse, whereas I can easily imagine one woman being turned on by another woman. The idea of rape doesn't arise when two women have sex, but I think it's present constantly in sex between two men.

The Uranian and Lunar components that form my character operate at another level, without being contradictory. I have a great need for women; I always need to feel one at my side, because I'm very close to them.

If all my affairs (even the shortest ones) have been satisfactory—and I don't mean only in sexual terms, but also in emotional terms—it's been because of my total understanding of women. I can satisfy all their desires and that, if I may say so, is a sign of great virility. All virile men are close to the female world . . . in bed.

I love women, but I prefer the company of men. Men, among themselves, are more fun and their topics of conversation more varied: sports, politics, sex. Men talk about the Tour de France, boxing, horse racing, soccer, billiards, women—all of which are hard to discuss with a woman, even if she's crazy about bicycles and horses. She's always waiting for somebody to ask her for a date, or pay her a compliment, or propose marriage. What's more, I find that women themselves show a preference for masculine company—even out of bed. Men are pleasanter and more straightforward. And on this score, too, I ask history to speak for the jealous, wily, underhanded, or naïve nature of our mates.

Women have always had to fight with unequal arms, since women are weaker physically. So they deploy a panoply of shrewdness, trickery, craftiness, perfidiousness, and wile that throws all relations between the sexes out of kilter.

[*This avalanche of "modifiers" aimed our way, girls, is somewhat mitigated by the astrologer, to whom I give the pen once more.—M.-T.G.*]

"He can gamble; he can use trickery; he can justify any of his behavior, but he actually remains sincere even when he uses trickery.

"On the other hand, he gambles with his *I*, he gears down his *I*.

"Building a future with a man like him is a bad bet for a woman. But what charm! What seductiveness! What power he transmits to his mate! He's a midwife of souls. If a woman is asleep, he wakes her. An awakener—I think that's the key word with him. With him, you turn a page and everything must begin over, everything must be re-examined.

"His health can withstand anything; he has enormous vitality, but he lives on his nervous tension. I think he's predisposed to wear and tear. At fifty, he will feel rather weary.

"He gives me the feeling that he so identifies with the values of youth and speed that I can hardly picture him as a little old man sitting on a bench resting both hands on the handle of his cane. Yet he has many years ahead of him—and good years.

"From the financial point of view, there will be great ups and downs.

"The big dates in his life: 1960 was a very favorable period and so was 1961; 1958 and 1959 having been years in which he got under way, his reputation had already been made. The present period is made of difficulty and struggle. In the area of his career, I see an improvement in 1971 and the years that follow will be even more favorable but it's changing.

"What characterizes the years '72, '73, '74 is access to maturity with transformations in his personality and then positive development. He goes on acting, but he sets foot in another world.

"Beginning in the spring of 1975—I can pinpoint the period—he goes into an extraordinarily favorable run. Nineteen seventy-six, '77, '78 constitute the most favorable phase of his whole life, which is in full swing in 1978. That will be the peak and then this will continue in 1979 and until 1980.

"His good luck doesn't end there—I still see something very big toward 1985.

"This is how I define the general curve, and all the dates that I have given, all their meanings, are certain.

"Before these years, '75-'78, which will be years of output, success, fullness, there are the years that come before, years of conversion and transformation. Perhaps an evolution will take place. That's why I am unable to specify the area in which this new success will appear.

"In the area of romance, he is currently in a rather favorable period, which should bring him a calming climate (to the extent that he can be calm).

"I foresee an important sentimental stage in the summer of 1972. I have the feeling that he will stick with a partner. He is capable of sticking for a certain time.

"Can I say if this is good or if it's bad? That depends on him, on the level he's at, on the stage he's at. If he's stayed with values a bit too close to adolescence, he stands a chance of spoiling his possibilities; if, on the contrary, he has acquired true emotional maturity, he tends to stay with one woman, something that enables him to continue an evolution in a real and deep relationship.

"He wants to live at home, which leads me to think that he wants married life, and I think he's taking that course. He has a tendency to develop his emotional life and to develop it in the direction of a certain maturation."

11.

IT'S TRUE THAT, BACK IN THOSE DAYS, I felt the need
to live at home. It's true that I didn't feel like living there alone, since I moved into an apartment on the
Boulevard d'Auteuil, in Boulogne, a suburb of Paris.

The apartment was a big one. I had it decorated, but
there was no furniture, or almost none. I wanted my "wife"
to pick it out. A woman must be able to compose the background of her life, I thought. . . . The apartment is still
empty, or almost so. I have organized only my personal living space: my bedroom and my bathroom.

The rooms intended for my future children—I'd hoped to
have them—are used by my mother and father when they
stop in Paris. And by my ex-wife, too.

It's true that the years 1968–69 were full of pitfalls.

Released from the contract that had bound me to Columbia, I became one of the best-paid actors in the world. Everything led me to hope, but—oh, those *buts!*—Hollywood
was in a severe slump. I worked for producers (French ones,
among others) who, with the exception of Verneuil and a
handful of others, didn't enjoy big international distribution.
Their budgets were geared accordingly and, hence, my salary too. These disappointments seldom coming alone, my
new passion, horses, would bring me new ones.

In 1966, I was to make *The Night of the Generals* in Poland, with Peter O'Toole.

A few days before my departure I bumped into Raphaël Hakim. Raphaël Hakim is a friend. He told me how he'd just bought a horse: "Do you want half of it?" I didn't spend much time thinking it over: "Okay." I gave him a check and I went away.

So that's how I became co-owner of a horse, a filly, baptized Slata. I vaguely wondered what she looked like. I wasn't going to find out until I got back to Paris.

I learned that Slata would be running at Longchamp. I went to see her. She looked like the other horses, with her red coat, her delicate, nervous legs. Slata was just one more race horse among all the others. I looked at her without particular feeling, but it just so happened that she won that day. And again a month later. She finished among the first three in two other races—then she died.

I was caught in the trap. Still partners with Hakim, I bought four or five other yearlings that weren't successful, but I'd caught the bug. I broke the Hakim-Sharif partnership and went out on my own. It was a great adventure.

Why this sudden passion? How should I know?

I'd always been fond of horses. Deep-rooted in me, there must be that image known to every child raised in the East: the man who rides a horse is strong. As a teen-ager, I rode. But there's a big jump from that horseback riding to a time when I'd be out at the stables before sunrise. At any rate, I went to Deauville for the annual sale of yearlings. It cost plenty for a yearling, but I felt like gambling on a few of them.

I built up an embryonic stable, all my own, and began training my horses. All I had to do then was make my entrance into the racing world. I had to have my colors, and that was no simple matter. The circle of owners was tightly

In Le Casse *with Jean-Paul Belmondo and Robert Hossein.*

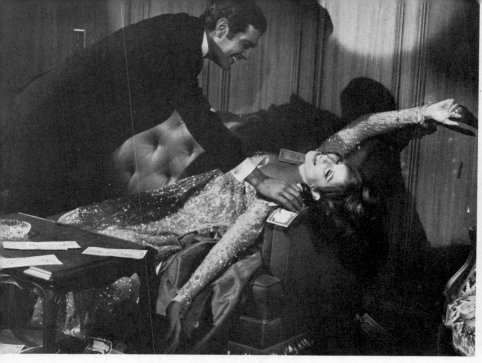

With Barbra Streisand in Funny Girl.

In Funny Girl.

With Karen Black in Crime and Passion.

In Crime and Passion, *directed by Ivan Passer, with Karen Black.*

closed. It didn't open easily—even though, in the last ten years, the lock that kept the door closed has been oiled slightly. I know.

I also know that the committee, which examines applications for admission, can turn down an applicant without having to state its reason for the rejection. I tried my luck. Quite soon I received a favorable reply. My jockeys would ride wearing pink and black, with black caps. That was back in 1967.

My horses scored a few victories. How could I resist? I expanded my stable. I invested plenty of money. Then Lady Luck turned her back on me. I went through the rough years predicted by my astrologer.

Was it because I believed in him? Have I followed my realistic nature? I can't say, but I did an about-face and went into horse breeding. I sold my males, I set up my fillies in Normandy and Ireland and learned the pleasures of the breeder.

It all started with the selection of the stallions. I learned by experience all the factors governing this difficult choice. First of all, questions of blood. These are of prime importance. I studied the strains; I analyzed performances. It was a game that I played very diligently. I was taught how to gauge the size of a stallion in comparison to the filly. A little mare must be mated with a large male if you want their offspring to be of normal size. That's logical.

I made the same calculations for the bones. Did I see a weakness in one side of the right hind leg? Wasn't it simply a question of making a more thorough examination of the father's—or mother's—legs?

Once these questions had been raised, I tried to solve them. You think you've worked out the answer, but heredity (which isn't so simple) often comes into play—most of all, the mother's heredity, which generally has greater impact than the father's. Then all my fine calculations were knocked for a loop. I would start in again from scratch. My alchemy had to be done over. With each crossing, my hopes rose. Disappointments came frequently, but I kept on.

Like all breeders, I dreamed of producing champions, thoroughbreds, and I was drawn to this dream even more because it seemed so hard. Was it my need to win, to conquer? I don't know whether horse breeding implies a winner's temperament or stems from a Ram or Taurus influence. I only know that I have mares and colts that I'm going to see born and frisk about, and that I'm going to enjoy it.

Why should we always look for psychological explanations for everything? To my mind, there's no psychological reason for anything. When you love jam, there's no psychological reason for it. You love jam, and that's that. Obviously, you can find a Freudian or Jungian explanation for liking jam. Why not? But it does seem pretty stupid.

Trying to figure out why you like jam, why you like horses, why you like money, why you like wine—all that drives me crazy. The only thing that counts is the love I feel momentarily for someone or something. Life would be too complicated if we went around constantly trying to figure out why we did one thing instead of another. Or why we didn't do it.

That's the way it is for me. I love something or I don't. At the time, I loved horses, I loved to breed them and I still breed them. I choose a father, a mother, and I wait for the offspring. It's a science, a pleasure that horse owners should approach with greater enthusiasm. In France, not enough is done to regenerate the blood of race horses.

It's true that, on top of breeding problems, monetary considerations come into the picture. A covering runs me from three thousand to two hundred thousand francs, sometimes more. I once paid twenty million old francs. And it didn't produce results.

You also have to figure on the cost involved in transporting the mares. The best stallions are scattered over the United States, England, and France. Depending on the stallion I've selected, I send my fillies to America, Great Britain, or to some French stud farm.

Today I own eight mares and many colts. In five years, from 1970 to 1975, I scored only three victories with three horses, in important races: one mare, Pink Pearl, who also gave me a colt that's presently in training; Blinis, who became a stud in southwestern France; and Royaltex, a horse that I was forced to part with because he suffered from a heart condition. These were the best that I ever had. Their descendants are in Ireland and in Normandy. I await their performances like an anxious father pacing back and forth outside the maternity ward.

As this maternity ward is set in the green meadows of Eire and of the Auge region of France, my anxiety is matched by my enchantment. I'm not exactly a nature lover. I never bother to go and see some particular scenery just because someone tells me it's beautiful. But when it happens to be staring me right in the face I do get pleasure from looking at it. So foaling time in Ireland and Normandy is always a happy event. . . . And yet I know from experience that horses aren't terribly affectionate animals. I don't expect them to whinny with happiness every time they see me.

Some people go to great lengths to caress a horse, while I'm convinced that this animal doesn't like being caressed. Actually, horses recognize only the groom who takes care of them, because he brushes them, currycombs them, feeds them.

Nor do I think that the horse is a terribly intelligent creature. But he is a noble beast. "Man's noblest conquest," as the saying goes.

For the rest, I place my trust in my trainers. Three years' experience doesn't make an accomplished horse breeder. It took me five more years to learn to size up a good match, largely because I can't ride my horses. I'm too heavy for the frail race horses. I'd have to weigh twenty-five pounds less than I do. And, in view of my height and build, that's hopeless.

So between two shootings I go and see my horses in Normandy and Ireland. I even go to Morocco, where I have a horse that was given to me by the King.

I was in Agadir on the same day that Hassan II happened to be there. He sent a message to me: "His Majesty has expressed the desire to see you." I made no attempt to figure out the reason for this royal desire, and I went to the golf course, which had been picked as our meeting place.

I met the King on the green and followed him around the course, chatting about this and that. We must have talked horses because at one point the King said, "Do you like horses? Go into my stables in Rabat and pick one out, any time you like."

From among many very fine animals, I selected a filly named Yasmina. Why that horse and not some other? Perhaps because of the little Princess' name. And that's undoubtedly the reason why I left her in Morocco.

Yasmina is still there. She grazes on grass that isn't so green as Normandy's or Ireland's, but I still have no plans for adding her to my stable.

I'm at every race at which my horses compete, but I never bet. For two reasons: first, because in 1970, following an unfortunate and very costly evening spent at the Casino de Deauville, I eliminated all games of chance from my activities; secondly, because in France betting is looked down on in horse-owning circles. Owners practically never bet and, if they do, it's through an intermediary. In England, on the other hand, it's traditional to bet. In Great Britain a gambler is considered a sportsman. In France he's a speculator, a rather shady individual. Ask any French banker if he'd lend money to gamblers.

The recent scandals that have rocked horse racing have given the sport a bad name. A few hoodlums stir up the greed of some jockeys who stupidly let themselves be corrupted and fall into the trap. The owners, the breeders, and even the regular jockeys emerge unscathed from these episodes, and when I meet them again they display the same serenity, the same dignity.

12.

IN MOUNTING MY HORSES, I skipped over years I'd like to cover at an easier pace.

Thus, there was *The Night of the Generals,* linked to the purchase of my first "half of a horse." This film brought me close to the horrors of Nazism in the countries ravaged by Hitler. In it I played a German policeman in charge of investigating the murder of a prostitute which had involved a Nazi general (Peter O'Toole). Obviously, Spiegel was trying to re-create the *Lawrence of Arabia* billboard. It's not hard to understand his reasons.

Being with Peter again delighted me, but wearing a German uniform struck me as incompatible with my physique and character. "It's grotesque," was my first reaction. The director, Anatole Litvak, insisted: "Let's do a little test." And the test proved fairly convincing. My mustache re-shaped, the uniform made me into a different man.

It was January. We were shooting in the streets of Warsaw. It was bitter cold. Between shots I walked into a little café, wearing my costume. I'd just wanted a cup of coffee and hadn't even thought about the uniform. I looked around and what did I see? Panic-stricken faces, people with tears welling up in their eyes.

"I'm no German!" I yelled quickly. "I'm making an American movie. I'm an American."

I even usurped a nationality to help reassure them. Nobody said a word. The barman refused to serve me. I suddenly understood the incongruity of that German uniform in a peaceful neighborhood café. I sensed the sadness that it inspired. I went out in dismay.

The next day, out of curiosity, I went back to the little café between shots, still dressed up in that damn uniform, and I met with the same refusal and provoked the same consternation.

Twenty-two years had elapsed without mitigating the pain and horror. On that day I learned that time can't make people forget.

We stayed in Warsaw for a month, constantly in German uniform. Even I, who hadn't gone through the Nazi invasion, learned to hate them.

And time was still going by . . . too fast to suit me when I was in Paris.

The interiors of *The Night of the Generals,* filmed in the Paris studios, were hardly done when one—no, two—contracts took me back to Hollywood: *Mackenna's Gold,* a western, the only one of my career, and *Funny Girl* would keep me stuck there for a year. I rented a villa in Beverly Hills and urged my family to come. I had been divorced from Faten but she was my best friend.

There I was, a father for the first time. A father in the emotional sense of the word but also in the possessive sense. Tarek was going on eleven and our relationship had been chopped up into so many successive phases by my stays in Cairo. We loved each other, Tarek and I, but we didn't know how to express this affection. I said to myself that living under the same roof for a few months would enable us to get back to the way it had been during his early childhood, when a cozy family atmosphere had established bonds that I wanted to knit together again.

There had been the rift caused by *Lawrence of Arabia*—two years during which I'd missed Tarek. Faten told me how he would play my favorite records over and over. After *Lawrence*, he listened endlessly to the theme music from the film. *Doctor Zhivago* brought us together again. For two months we both lived exclusively for each other. I put him to sleep in my bed and I would lie down next to him. I ate all my meals with him; I didn't go out, so that he wouldn't be left home alone. We lived together twenty-four hours a day. That was a wonderful period. Tarek was seven and a half; he was like a flower slowly opening up to life; he hardly emerged from his cocoon to move in my world, the world of movies. It was exciting. . . .

Afterward we were separated again. For Tarek, that meant a boarding school in Switzerland; for me, running up and down two continents in front of cameras. I rarely had time off when he was on vacation, so we slipped back into that episodic relationship of ours, kept alive by a few childish letters that brought back a memory, nothing more.

Nevertheless, my influence on him grew and grew. He would refuse to obey his mother but he'd yield without argument to my decisions, and the last of these decisions masked an intense desire: "Come and stay with me in Hollywood with your mother."

So it was that, on a day in July of 1967, after a tough day's shooting, marked, as I recall, by a slight accident—one of Gregory Peck's badly aimed punches landed smack on my nose—I came home to find Faten, Tarek, Nadia (Faten's daughter), Pepita (the governess), and Starlight (my son's hideous little poodle).

Tarek had been adamant: "If Starlight doesn't go, I don't go."

Pepita had taken it on herself to stuff the dog in an over-night bag and hide him from the customs officers, so as to avoid the baggage compartment. The trick worked. Tarek told me that during the eleven-hour flight Starlight had been out of the bag, sitting quietly between Pepita and him. Whenever the stewardess went by the dog would bury his head in the hollow of the seat. It became a game—he seemed perfectly aware of the irregularity of his situation. Starlight hadn't had anything to drink or eat; he hadn't relieved himself once throughout the flight, but as soon as he got off at the Los Angeles airport he went racing toward the nearest tree—almost losing his freedom in so doing.

At last they were with me. I'd had roast chicken prepared (at the time, Tarek loved chicken). I'd also had his favorite desserts made ready. Around a table laden with flowers, we began the meal in a festive atmosphere. But then Tarek picked up a chicken leg with his fingers. I turned livid with rage. I was so overwhelmed by anger that I knocked over the table and sent my son to bed without supper. Our reunion was a fiasco. I'd been spoiled, but I'd also been brought up very strictly. So I took out that strictness on my son. He didn't show it the next day, but something had come between us.

Tarek discovered the United States with amazement. America was a children's paradise. All day long the TV set broadcast adventure and gangster movies, cartoons, special shows for kids. There were all these automatic gadgets that swallowed coins and spewed candy, cookies, bottles of Coca-Cola, hot dogs, hamburgers, oatmeal, cornflakes. There were skyscrapers. From the hundredth floor you could see people reduced to the size of insects running around in toy towns. It was fun. There were the wonderful elevators. I remembered that, when my parents had moved us into a twelfth-floor apartment, I was wildly excited. And then there were Disneyland, Marineland, zoos, and Lunaparks. There was everything.

Tarek was enchanted by the United States. He even planned to go to an American college. But his enchantment wasn't anything compared to Pepita's.

Since 1965, Pepita had been my son's governess. She's been my housekeeper since Tarek went to school in England and Faten took up residence there. Pepita couldn't stand the London fog so she came over to Paris to run my house.

In Hollywood, Pepita was to spend the vacations with my son. But we hadn't counted on her Spanish sense of duty: "The cook doesn't know how to make the gentleman's breakfast, so I'll make it myself."

So, the day after her arrival, Pepita was in the kitchen at the crack of dawn and on hand, at 7:00 A.M., when I left for the studio. A big car stopped in front of the villa, a chauffeur got out, opened the door for me, and off we went. Ten minutes later Pepita saw an identical limousine drive up to the house. She woke up my secretary.

"The gentleman has forgotten something—come quick."

My secretary pulled on a bathrobe, went out, looked at the automobile and, stifling a yawn, said, "That isn't the gentleman's car. It's the cook's."

Pepita was aghast, skeptical. A cook couldn't have the same car as her employer—that was impossible. This equality in life styles hadn't struck me. I'd seen nothing wrong. I needed Pepita's astonishment to make me notice it.

Pepita had further cause for surprise.

The Hollywood chauffeur whom the studio assigns to me when I'm making a picture is Mexican, so he speaks Spanish. At that time he happened to be working for Elvis Presley, whose villa was adjacent to mine. I begged to have him back, thinking that he could serve as squire to Pepita, who didn't speak a word of English. . . . I got him back.

Ignacio dazzled her in two respects: he had a fine build and a splendid Mustang convertible. Ignacio showed her Los Angeles night life; she went to the night clubs of the stars, she ate creamed sole sprinkled with Coca-Cola (it's quite popular in America).

And then one day she announced her forthcoming marriage to Ignacio. And then Ignacio didn't come by with his Mustang to pick her up any more in the evening, and Pepita was sad.

Faten became worried and asked, "What is it?"

"I had him investigated and they told me that he's already got three wives and five children," answered Pepita in tears. Disappointed, deceived, she went back to Paris with Tarek and Nadia three months later. Faten, bound by contract to Cairo, stayed only two weeks.

As for my son, I hadn't really been able to get together with him. The free time I'd been hoping for had been whittled down to a few suppers together. That wasn't enough to get a flame out of the smoldering embers.

Things didn't click until three years later, when he'd become a teen-ager. I had just moved into a Paris apartment. Tarek was going to a "public" school in London but spent all his vacations with me in Paris and Deauville. He loved France right away and he loved Deauville, and he was always willing to visit me there. He began writting real letters —happy, funny ones. I discovered that my son had a sense of humor and I was delighted. He would write about himself and the people around him, explaining how he'd washed his socks for the first time: "Soap and water aren't as easy to handle as you might think; you've got to add some elbow grease, but if you see this exercise as sport, it all becomes funny. But don't get the idea that I'm going to replace the cleaning lady during vacations."

He wrote about his friends, their foibles, their likable

sides: "I was asked to play Romeo with a girl I didn't like so I refused. . . . Juliet is fat—can you imagine a love scene with a fat girl?"

He would tell me stories, then phone me to comment on them, and each letter, each phone call brought us closer. . . . One day he told me about his first flirt. The age of puberty was there! His muscles had grown hard, the hair on his body was developing, his voice had become deeper. I was watching myself grow up. I recalled the feelings I'd had long before. I was reliving my youth. And this made it easier for us to get together. Not father and son, but two pals, despite the respect and admiration that Tarek had for me.

Is this because I encouraged the friendly side of our relationship? Today, Tarek consults me on everything: the way he dresses, his girl friends, his reading, sports, everything.

One day, as I was coming into the Paris apartment, I passed a girl who wasn't very pretty. "Your girl friend is homely," I said later. Tarek made no comment, but I never saw that girl again.

He doesn't talk much and, when he does, he speaks with modesty. He doesn't display his state of mind any more than I do. Though raised in Europe, my charming young fellow has the behavior of a Middle Easterner. He's the absolute counterpart of his father. Like me, he deliberately throws off any female hold on him—even that of his mother, whom he nevertheless adores. It's true that she doesn't speak French or English very well and that Tarek won't speak Arabic. He understands that language quite well but refuses to speak it. When his mother and I try to encourage him in conversation in Arabic, he answers us in either French or English.

My son's "philosophy" is my own. It's a way of being that consists of letting yourself live, profiting from each passing instant, without trying to figure out the implications of that instant on the instant that comes after it. It's fairly simplistic and stems from a healthy egotism, and yet I think I can safely state that Tarek and I have generous natures. How many young actors, how many friends have I helped? I don't know. But I am certain that, each time, I did it willingly. Because they were physically present. And only when they were present. As soon as they moved away, I must admit, any assistance from me ended automatically. I didn't have the time or the desire to follow them in their endeavors elsewhere.

Like my son, I concern myself with what is right around me. This holds true for politics and world upheaval. I have to be in contact with the events, with the people. To be concerned, I must see and hear and listen. Distant happenings can't touch me; they don't affect me personally. They don't touch the exact people where I am, so I can't be part of those events. They take place far away and I don't see them with my own eyes.

The Nasserian revolution failed to move me because I didn't really see it happen. I said earlier that the revolution took place in the wee hours of the morning and that it lasted a few hours. When I came out of my house I walked through the streets just as I had the day before, saw people who were talking to one another about the revolution. Sure, it was big news, but nothing in my everyday life changed. The people were talking to one another in the streets of Cairo—and they're still doing it.

Both my son and I are a bit like people who work, people whose world is limited to the factory, the office, or the home. My own world is my home, studios, and night clubs. As long as events fail to change my personal world I remain unaware of them.

Some people are concerned about the world. I'm not one of them. I don't belong to the "committed intellectual" group. All theories, all great ideas fill me with fear. So many of these theories and great ideas have wound up causing horrible conflicts and atrocious massacres that I have a deep-seated fear of them. Christ's preachings were good and fine. But how many crimes have been committed in his name?

Tarek got through the student unrest of 1968. The clamor of the demonstrations could not penetrate the perfectly insulated walls of English "public" schools. But had he spoken to me in slogans straight from the barricades I would have understood him. How can we expect young people to remain passive in the face of wars, atrocities, injustice? How are they to go on like that, if we can't provide them with rational explanations (to the extent that there are any)?

But let's say (and now I speak strictly as a father) that it's more comfortable to be the father of a son who isn't mixed up in radical student movements. Likewise, I'm glad that Tarek has accepted the material comfort that I've offered him. But at no time have I ever forced him to accept it.

What do I expect from him? He's going to carry on where I left off. He's just entered the London Academy Theater. After a great deal of hesitation, he wants to find out if he's got what it takes to be an actor. But I certainly had something to do with his decision, and neither of us is convinced about his vocation.

At sixteen he planned to go into the business world. He talked about spending his summer vacations with his grandfather, to learn the timber business. My father was overjoyed. Me? I was dumfounded. The idea of a sixteen-year-old kid who didn't dream of being a pilot or an actor, a kid who didn't want to conquer the world—this I couldn't understand. At his age I thought about "doing things." I thought about leaving home, meeting people, learning, seeing, doing! I wanted to be something else, to be somebody—an actor, a movie star, a mathematician, an inventor. I wanted to be everything all at once. And there was my boy, with an ambition to find the cubic footage of a log and to make a few bucks per cubic yard or per board foot! What the hell kind of an ambition was that?

An easy, comfortable, luxurious life—that satisfied Tarek, and I sometimes wonder if he hasn't just one aim: to get himself luxury and comfort via motion pictures.

Now, in my case, I wasn't able to continue working in legitimate theater because my need for money grew with each passing year. But I'd like him to be a great actor on the stage. The theater is the place where an actor realizes his potential most completely. That's where an actor's presence counts. Facing his audience, it's stage presence alone that wins or loses.

I miss the stage, and I'd love to return through Tarek. But I realize that great ambitions can't be directed—especially where show business is concerned.

I reached the peak of my career between 1969 and 1970. My astrologer's predictions came true year after year, at the tempo he'd foreseen.

The Last Valley and *The Horsemen* made me some money. Just before those, I did four pictures with the relish of a young wolf about to devour the carrion he's gathered. I'd just been released from the contract binding me to Columbia. At last I was going to reap the fruits of my popularity and my work.

Starting with *Mayerling*, things began improving financially. We were on location in Austria with the wonderful Ava Gardner. I became her friend: someone who showed her affection, took her out, showered her with attention.

Ava is a lonely person. She's one of those people perpetually frustrated in love because they're too demanding. Terrific guys have been in love with her, but they couldn't satisfy her need for the absolute and Ava was always disappointed. She has known glory, wealth, but never love in the sense that she understood it: total giving shared in passion.

Infinitely feminine, Ava doesn't like women, of course, so I was her squire for three months. We struck up a rather ambiguous, highly pleasurable camaraderie, one that bordered on romance.

Only alcohol made her lighthearted, only alcohol could relax her. She needed to drink to drown her sorrows, and in this respect Ava was a lot like Rita Hayworth. They resembled each other, they ran into the same problems that neither one of them could solve. They led the same kind of life, were equally beautiful, had the same understanding of things, the same unsatisfied need to live in great passion. They're often compared to Marilyn Monroe. Wrongly. I think Marilyn was basically lacking stability . . . so she cracked up earlier.

On the set, Ava Gardner the actress forgot Ava Gardner the woman. She would take charge of a part with extraordinary self-assurance. Quite unlike Ingrid Bergman, whom I'd had as a co-star in *The Yellow Rolls-Royce*, which was also filmed in Austria.

At first sight Ingrid gave me the impression of being an ordinary woman, such was her simplicity. Wholesome, likable, warm, even-tempered, kind, co-operative, she had an easygoing manner that was unusual in a movie star.

Face to face with her on the set for the first time, I realized how tall she was. On the screen she'd seemed small, gentle, tender, and there she was so tall beside me. I was almost aghast. Her bone structure wasn't feminine, and neither was her walk. A slight timidity made her awkward. She spoke badly, groping for words. I said to myself, "This girl doesn't know her lines, she isn't any good. . . ." And then the next day, screening the rushes, I thought her style was admirable for its restraint, for the precision of her expression, and I realized that her talent was inside. It was as though the eye couldn't perceive it directly and needed the camera to give its true dimension.

Ingrid Bergman, the actress (she's a real actress in the noble sense of the word), thrilled me. Ingrid Bergman, the woman, captivated me. She seemed perfect. Her great height, which could have been a handicap, was good for one thing at least: to compensate for it, Ingrid had to develop her femininity. And I'm thankful to that heavy bone structure, to those inches too many which brought us that incomparable gentleness. Her eyes express all the tenderness in the world. The color of her cheeks heightens at the right moment. What a delight for a man like me who loves women who blush!

She was wonderful. I fell in love with her. I dragged her out to the race tracks. She wasn't mad about horses but went with me, just to please me, and tried loyally to take an interest in racing because I was interested in it.

In Austria, I went through an experience: I felt like a foreigner in a foreign land. And I knew why! It was a language problem. I wasn't used to being unable to communicate with people. My total ignorance of German and the Slavic languages puts a curtain around the Eastern European countries for me—not an iron curtain, but one that's solid nonetheless. I tried to raise that curtain at the time of *Zhivago,* for not being able to read Pasternak in Russian bothered me.

The Austrian has a rather clever side, one that's even likable. He is cultivated, sophisticated, a lover of music and art. Vienna, his capital, is so beautiful. Had I been a grownup at the turn of the century, I would have chosen to live there. . . . Today, Vienna is dying. . . .

In May 1968, France was crippled by strikes. I was in Juan les Pins on the Côte d'Azur, where only faint echoes of the student revolt reached us.

One day I was playing in a bridge tournament when two dusty, haggard-looking creatures climbed out of a big car with German license plates. They wanted to see me. It was Darryl Zanuck and the American director Richard Fleischer.

Three times before they'd offered me the part of Che Guevara. I'd turned it down three times. They were making another attempt.

"We've come all the way from Germany to convince you that nobody but you can play Che."

I used the arguments I'd already developed. "It's a bad bet, making a picture about a contemporary hero. But to have the film made by the very people the hero was fighting —the Americans—means guaranteeing a flop."

The legends and gods set up by young people must be taken into account by film makers. Mr. Zanuck didn't exactly follow the revolutionary line. He represented the very capitalistic enterprise Twentieth Century-Fox, whose interests were closely connected to those of the American government.

I made myself more explicit. "I refuse to make a rightist movie about a leftist hero."

I wanted to respect Che Guevara's character. I liked Che a lot. I'd read everything that had been written about him. I'd met people who had known him. He seemed eminently worthy of respect. Not necessarily for his convictions and his political actions, which one might or might not accept, but for his sincerity and his incorruptibility. I admire incorruptibility. It's an important trait that's rarely found. I said to myself: "Human beings are naturally corruptible; money corrupts them." I'd come across a man who couldn't be corrupted and I wasn't going to betray him. Everyone knows that I'm neither leftist nor rightist, but risk betraying the image and ideal of a revolutionary hero? No, that I couldn't do.

Zanuck persuaded me that the picture would be fair and unbiased, so for the first time in the history of Hollywood motion pictures a conscience clause was written into my contract. It gave me the right to examine the film from the political standpoint. I was entitled to refuse shooting any scene that didn't seem consistent with the facts.

I signed and we left for Puerto Rico, where the lush vegetation made it possible to re-create Cuba's Sierra Maestra. Then the arguments started. Back and forth, I'd send my observations to the producer and I'd get back his, which I didn't like.

The set became a forum where endless discussions went on, discussions that grew more violent with each passing day. When I wasn't in front of the camera I watched what was happening behind my back. This incessant struggle proved to be exhausting and, I must confess, ineffectual. While I did manage to save the legend of Che and kept it intact, the character of Fidel Castro became a laughing stock. It was all perfectly idiotic: they turned Castro into a grotesque stooge following in Che Guevara's wake. They depicted him as an idiot who had to consult with Che before taking the slightest step forward in a revolution which had actually been his doing. Fidel Castro is courageous, intelligent, honest, and this in no way detracts from the legendary exploits of the CIA's victim.

But Cuba is too close to the United States. The results weren't long in coming. After a three-day run at a large movie theater in New York the film had to be taken off the

program. Crowds of young people had shown their disapproval noisily. At any rate, there wasn't a seat left intact for
the audiences.

Che! met the same fate wherever it was shown. . . .
Never had a motion picture cost its distributors so many
seats.

13.

I WAS PLAYING IN A BRIDGE TOURNAMENT at Juan les Pins when Fleischer came after me to do *Che!*

I'd just set up the first world tournament team, which had grown out of great feelings: friendship, esteem, admiration for my three partners, and our love for bridge.

My uncle loved bridge and had introduced me to the game, but it wasn't until the age of twenty-one that I really learned to play. I was making my first picture in Cairo. Between shots, just to pass the time, I used to read, and that's when I came across a book on how to play bridge. I couldn't put it down. I was already hooked on mental gymnastics, like crossword and jigsaw puzzles; now I added bridge.

It was the bidding system developed by Charles H. Goren, the man who popularized the game the world over.

In the early 1930s Ely Culbertson and his wife Josephine had challenged the whole bridge world in tournaments with very high stakes. They played for money, and two matches, which they won, have gone down in the annals of bridge. The Culbertson system of contract bridge was firmly established by the middle thirties.

In 1949, Goren devised his bidding system. He was one of the good players but not the best. His partner, Helen Sobel, was to the best of my knowledge the only woman who has equaled men in playing skill. The couple became famous but their names were unknown in Europe until the appearance of Goren's first book, a bridge self-teacher. At the time Pierre Albarran was the foremost authority on bridge in France. He was the French Culbertson.

Goren scored a tremendous breakthrough with his point-count system, which may have borrowed from Culbertson's but it's simplified, within the reach of all. In his books, bridge players find all their questions answered in clear, concise language. I know what I'm talking about because I learned to play by reading his first book. And I've never taken a single lesson. But I did pay a high price while putting Goren's teachings into practice. Right away, I got in with the best players and, sure enough, they trounced me every time. I was interesting neither as an adversary or a teammate, but they accepted me because the stakes were high and they won plenty of money from me. That was the price I had to pay to learn. The lessons were expensive but effective, because one day I was picked to take part in the World Bridge Olympiad, in New York, with the three best Egyptian players. I must admit that they were of average skill compared to the other international champions. But it was a start. Today (and this is no small feat) I can take on the most accomplished forty or fifty bridge players in the world.

In 1968, Benito Garozzo, Giorgio Belladonna, and Pietro Forquet were undefeated at the international championships. I played with them several times in friendly games but not in competition, because the teams are national. They were Italian and I was Egyptian. Egypt couldn't muster four international-level bridge players, so I had to come up with a solution. I borrowed the idea of tennis pros and set up a professional tournament team. Why? To play more often with champions, and to interest the public in a game that I found subtle and complex. I didn't hire

my friends full time, but I organized tournaments in the
United States and Europe, for which I assumed all the ex-
penses.

Garozzo is a jeweler in Milan, Belladonna a civil servant
in the Italian government, Forquet a bank officer in Naples.
They were the first bridge pros in the world—and they had
not given up their usual occupations.

The tournaments are held in big hotels, before six or
seven hundred spectators when they take place in America,
and before four or five hundred people on the continent of
Europe. Some of these spectators are bridge fans, others are
women who come to see Omar Sharif. But there aren't any
run-of-the-mill people. Obviously, I have used my popularity to draw crowds to the bridge tables. The games are
shown in their entirety in the hall via an electronic system
and reproduced over closed-circuit television. In this way
everyone can watch the game on a big screen.

The first year, we held a five-week tournament in North
America. The next year, again for five weeks, we traveled all
over Europe—mainly Holland, Belgium, and England, three
great bridge-loving countries. Each tournament represented
a test of endurance. For three (often four) hours we would
play. This was reported over television, radio, and in the
newspapers. Gradually boosters showed up, new boosters.
The professional team movement had been launched.

First to follow in my footsteps was a Texan who set up a
rival team, the Dallas Aces.

A Chinese shipowner, C. C. Wei, who had also been bit-
ten by the bug, offered my three associates sums of money
that I couldn't possibly match. I urged them to accept. Lancia, the Italian industrialist, outbid the Chinese fellow, and
that's how I got Garozzo, Belladonna, and Forquet back
under the Bridge Team Lancia flag. Our only obligation out-

side tournaments: we all had to drive Lancia cars. Which wasn't really that unpleasant. . . .

I have one great hope: to see other major brands of whiskey, detergent, or cars—anything—move into pro bridge. This game, which is loved by millions, provides a living for only five or six thousand people. My own teammates, who are still world champions, earn a living from bridge— unofficially, not officially. Like all other games, bridge requires long, hard training and a great deal of intelligence. Winning isn't a matter of luck. A winner doesn't just happen. He's more gifted than the others, he's quicker on the trigger, he can solve game problems.

Bridge is a language between two partners who can choose from among a host of tried and tested systems: standard basic, Standard American, Standard French. Each system has its own conventions, such as the Neapolitan Club, the Roman Club, the Polish Club, Chinese Precision, Italian Super-precision, Monaco, the Four-leaf Club. There are also all the systems which partners devise and use but which have no name.

A few specifics? Well, the Leghorn diamond indicates a strong hand. An opening bid with a club is an artificial call which, depending on the system, implies fifteen, sixteen, or seventeen points, while a natural call consists of opening in the dominant suit, independently of the strength of the hand.

But—and I want to stress this point—the use of secret codes between partners is absolutely forbidden at tournaments or championships. Before sitting down at a card table the teams must come to an agreement about a set of rules. A copy of the system used is in the bridge players' possession at the start of the game. "Confidential" bids (ones understood only by a partner) aren't allowed. Opponents would be playing fair in asking questions, in having the meaning of a bid made explicit, and the trick would be on those who tried to be clever (if not actually to cheat).

In the whole world there are only forty-odd champions. I'm one of them—I say this without conceit since I play against them regularly and, often, with success.

The Italian team, Squadra Azzurra, is the most famous one. International champions for fifteen years, the team roster includes my aforementioned tournament partners plus Walter Avarelli.

Among the Americans, I should mention Stone and Roth and the Dallas Aces, who are subsidized by a leading Texas financier. The Englishmen Terence Reese, Boris Schapiro, and Jeremy Flint are also crack players. As for the French, I'd put Svarc and Boulanger at the top of the list.

They all have certain things in common: a keen mathematical mind and great powers of concentration—the essential quantities of the bridge player. They have intuitive minds and vast experience.

Does this mean that bridge is only for intellectuals? No, absolutely not. You don't need a drawerful of diplomas to be a good bridge player. Most of all, the game calls for a certain turn of mind, the kind that enables you to solve enigmas, problems that change from one minute to the next. To be played properly, the game also calls for passion. Bridge, unlike poker, isn't based on luck, but on intelligence. It is the perfect game. What's more, it has come a long way from the drawing rooms of high society to the present-day bridge clubs open to anyone. When you sit down at a bridge table you don't ask to see your partner's résumé or your opponent's either. The only thing that counts: a person's playing skill. Good bridge players have a plain, straightforward style; they don't use trickery—just logic.

If there is any screening in the bridge clubs, it's geared to the person's freedom of movement rather than to the thickness of his wallet or his social and intellectual class. Competitions are extremely fast-paced, something that demands great physical endurance, as I've said, and plenty of free time. This may explain why there are so few women champions. Young women have homes that keep them busy; the older ones no longer have the stamina required. Unfortunately, the majority of women bridge players have passed the age where women get whistled at. When we realize that champions aren't usually over fifty and that they don't like to play with average players, women must necessarily remain in the game's minor leagues.

I've had two experiences—quite accidentally—that nearly turned out disastrously.

The first time was back in January 1967. I was in St. Moritz for the classic winter tournament, in which I was participating for the first time. I'd scarcely checked into my hotel when the phone rang. A voice introduced itself.

"I'm the Shah's secretary. His Majesty loves bridge—so does the Empress. She's just a beginner, but very excited by the game. They'd be happy if you could come over for a game at their chalet."

The wishes of emperors are commands.

"Very well," I answered.

The secretary made the date for two days later, a Tuesday, then went on to ask, "Is there something you'd particularly like to eat for dinner?"

"Yes, indeed. I love caviar and Persian rice."

My mother used to make it wonderfully and I've always retained a marked taste for Persian rice (and for rice in general)—when it's well prepared.

That Tuesday, at the appointed time, 8:00 P.M., a driver picked me up at my hotel. He dropped me off in front of a chalet located half an hour's ride from St. Moritz.

I received a warm welcome from the imperial couple and

from a Belgian ambassador stationed in some country I've forgotten, but whom I'd already met in a bridge club or at a tournament. I was sure that he was a bridge player.

We drank a glass of champagne, then went into the dining room. Farah Dibah, who lived up to her reputation for charm, got up from the table to transmit our requests to the cooks. The meal took place in a simple family atmosphere. The caviar, brought specially from Iran, was excellent; the Persian rice equaled my mother's.

Afterward, sitting down at the card table, I wondered—half in earnest, half in amusement—if I had the right to beat an emperor, if that was in keeping with the dictates of etiquette. . . . I don't remember whether the game went off in accordance with protocol, but one thing was certain—for a beginner, the Empress showed exceptional ability that reflected great intelligence.

At the end of the evening a large parcel was handed to me.

"Since you love it so much, here's fifty pounds of it." Fifty pounds of rice.

The second incident happened in Deauville four or five years ago. It began the same way—with a phone call. Around ten o'clock in the morning a voice announced:

"I am Maurice Schumann, Minister of Foreign Affairs. I'm wild about bridge, but I'm a rotten player—because I have so little time to practice. There is going to be a little tournament in Cabourg and I'd be pleased if you would join me there. You won't mind playing with an amateur, will you?"

"Well, er, no," I answered hypocritically.

"Then I'll come and get you at seven. We'll have supper together to work out our game plan. The tournament begins at nine."

I was a bit uneasy about all this, but I said to myself, "I'm going to stay calm, I'm going to be patient. After all, it's just a little beach resort tournament."

The supper went off pleasantly enough. Schumann's company was delightful, and we came to a hall where about twenty men and women, elderly for the most part, were sitting on little, uncomfortable chairs. Two armchairs had been reserved: one for the Minister of Foreign Affairs and the other for yours truly. It was embarrassing, but how could I swap my armchair for one of the old ladies' chairs?

The game began and I kept my decision firmly in mind: "Whatever he does, I won't blow up, I won't say a word, I'll be nice, I'll be patient."

We were playing the first deal and my partner made a huge blunder.

"But, Mr. Minister, why didn't you play your ace of diamonds?" I'd used a somewhat higher tone of voice than usual, but I hadn't blown my top.

"You're right, my good fellow, I should have. I thought of doing it—why *didn't* I do it?"

I couldn't be angry with him after that. I smiled. We were going into the second deal. This time his blooper was even bigger. I hardly mentioned it. Third deal. His mistake seemed enormous. I really began to get upset, my tone of voice grew sharp, I couldn't control myself. . . . At the end of the game I went berserk. I flung my cards down on the table and got up. . . . That's how I behaved with the Minister of Foreign Affairs, a charming, wonderfully pleasant man. . . . I only hope he's forgiven me, the bridge player, for what he would never have tolerated from me, the man.

After these experiences with amateurs, I'd like to recall a tournament that created a tremendous furor. It took place in

London. For a whole week we were competing against the Reese-Schapiro team. The BBC was covering the event.

Reese and Schapiro were accused of cheating. Brought to trial, both were acquitted. However, the Americans refused to play them. They had to be matched against other champions, backed by a huge publicity campaign, to get them back in the saddle. And they got back. Reese and Schapiro regained their rightful places in world competition. I've always been convinced that they were accused unjustly. This is often the tribute that the best must pay.

In 1971, I took part in another memorable game in England. Garozzo, Belladonna, and I had been challenged—for money—by Cansino and Flint, two British champions. The stakes were so high that this game was called "the most expensive game of the century." Fifty to a hundred million old francs were at stake. We'd accepted the challenge. Two pairs of players changed places at will with the third team-mate.

I personally accounted for about sixty per cent of the match. All Great Britain watched with bated breath. The bookmakers took bets. The results came out over TV and radio as well as in the newspapers. For the British, our match was as important as the Fischer-Spassky chess duels.

The big London hotel (I've forgotten the name) where our famous game took place was the focal point of interest for the entire nation. We played for a whole week, six hours a day—three in the afternoon, three in the morning. Very slowly, to satisfy the public.

Garozzo, Belladonna, and I finally defeated the English. But not by much, since we'd only won about ten million francs. In other words, the point spread was quite small.

Our Italian quartet has gone undefeated to this day.

Though it has been ten or twelve years since Goren played competitive bridge, he is still the most widely read of all bridge authorities. His organization, spearheaded by U.S. internationalist Harold Ogust, spends much time in continuing to popularize the game. More than two hundred newspapers and magazines the world over carry Goren articles. At regular intervals he adds another book to his long list of publications. He is the world's best-selling bridge author. His books have sold millions of copies and are translated into many languages. For instance, his point-count bidding system was the first bridge book ever translated into Hebrew! For the past two years my name has appeared as co-author with his on the syndicated column "Goren Bridge."

He also organized "Goren Cruises." Luxury liners sail from both the East and West coasts toward the islands of the Caribbean, Atlantic, or Pacific, or even around the world carrying bridge lovers who, for anything from one week to three months, polish their skills under the watchful eyes of Goren experts. Lessons and tournaments meet the needs of beginners and veteran players alike.

Goren and I have also co-operated in backgammon. This game, very popular in the United States for quite some time, is slowly taking root in other countries as well. Some of the finest clubs in Europe now include backgammon among their activities. Together, we have published a backgammon book in Europe and have manufactured backgammon boards for sale in Britain.

This association with Goren thrills me and proves (if proof is necessary) how much I love bridge and bridge players. My best friends play bridge. That's all we talk about. I don't know my partners or my opponents; I know nothing about their families, their love affairs, their thoughts. I only know that this one is an average player, that one is a good player, So-in-so is a champion, and I love talking about my last hand with that champion.

Games are always followed by a drink or supper—that's a pleasant way to prolong the game.

I'm often asked if this passion of mine for bridge is compatible with my acting career.

Isn't the characteristic feature of any passion its incompatibility with everyday life? Golf really isn't compatible with the life of an overworked businessman. Yet, if he likes it, he finds time to get out on the green. Bridge is a sport of the mind, it's a passion, an escape, a recreation, and for me, it's very important . . . So important that I'd cheerfully devote my life to it . . . But . . .

14.

IN 1969. I WAS DOING VERY WELL WITH MOVIES. Things were going so well that I didn't want to quit. They were handing me reams of clippings from the newspapers. The Sharif legend was born, a legend that the press kept alive. It's always good to get write-ups—that keeps my producers happy.

I was "the only really masculine lover" who's still young on the international screen, "the modern knight," "that Egyptian leaving a trail of conquests like something out of *A Thousand and One Nights*." I read these articles with mixed feelings: I was flattered by them (who wouldn't be?) but—was it really me? Was I that man decked out with descriptive adjectives in which I couldn't recognize myself? On the other hand, one article did say something that made a deep impression on me: "Omar Sharif, in demand everywhere for the last seven years, hasn't had a vacation." It was true.

Barely finished with *Che!*, I found myself back in Innsbruck, Austria, for *The Last Valley*, with Michael Caine and Florinda Bolkan, a superproduction that missed being a commercial success.

Then I left for Afghanistan to do *The Horsemen*, which was taken from the Joseph Kessel novel. John Frankenheimer didn't reach his target, the mass audience, but it remains a wonderful memory. My part—a barbarian horse-man—was thrilling. Three months of red-blooded adventure in the saddle. I brought back a fine Afghan hound, Baz (which means Eagle).

I was the first star to make a picture on location in that mountainous land, with its harsh climate, its arid soil, but its great beauty. Having learned somehow that I was there, the King sent for me. I went to the palace, where I was ushered into a little drawing room that was in no way ornate. All the books I'd read had misled me. Not every Eastern potentate lived like the maharajahs. The King was there. In European clothing. (Where were the flowing robes?) About fifty years old. He had a likable, friendly, almost humble way. We chatted over a cup of coffee. There was no ceremony in the way we conducted ourselves or the way we spoke. We kept switching back and forth from French into English. The King spoke both languages marvelously. He told me about his country's poverty and outlined his plans for coping with the problem. It was a pleasant, interesting conversation. At one point a dog came into the room and lay down at the feet of the person he seemed to recognize as his master. The dog was indescribably beautiful. I was carried away by my admiration for the animal. Forgetting the solemnity of our meeting, I broke in:

"Oh, Your Majesty, that's the finest-looking dog I've ever seen!"

"You like him? He's yours."

The response had been immediate. I was overwhelmed by embarrassment. I should never have made that comment. I should have remembered that in an Arab country the kind of remark I'd made amounted to "Give me the dog." I also knew that, once the blunder had been made, it was out of the question to refuse.

So Baz changed masters, just like that. Things became

more complicated when it came time to take him to Paris. Protocol (which had to be observed at that point) ruled out the possibility of sending the dog in the baggage compartment, where dogs normally travel. The palace reserved two first-class seats so that he might stretch out in comfort.

Taking off from Kabul, there was no problem about seating Baz. But I had to change planes in Teheran. So the management of Air France had to be notified about this VIP. Air France waived its regulations and assigned two seats to the royal dog that could then move in with me at Boulevard d'Auteuil.

Baz was coveted by all the other owners of Afghan hounds. Even Madame Pompidou "asked his hand in marriage" for her Afghan bitch that I didn't find as beautiful or pure of breed as Baz. (I felt the same way about most of the Afghan bitches that sighed over Baz in Deauville, where I took him each year.)

So it was that Baz died in 1974—without offspring.

I spoke of Baz coming to move in with me at Boulevard d'Auteuil. That did actually mark the first time I'd gone "home" after shooting a picture. So "home" was a word that I used to utter with a kind of delight.

I was thirty-seven years old and I'd settled down in Paris. Why Paris? That was something I just took for granted. For several reasons. I loved big cities. I couldn't even live in another French city or in Switzerland. My choice was narrow: London, Paris, or New York. New York? It was far, way too far from France. London—there was the handicap of weekends. London is dead from Friday to Monday morning. You've got to love the country. . . . And, anyway, hadn't I received a French education? At any rate, I'd always felt that I had. And Paris is such a beautiful city. You feel so free there. You can do anything you want, say whatever you think. There's no special racism in Paris. If there were any, a segment of the population would always clamor for tolerance.

So Paris adopted me twice. The first time—in 1963—just after the release of *Lawrence of Arabia*. In Hollywood, movie people "received me" the way they receive all new stars. In Paris, I had the good fortune to be "recognized" by certain intelligent, cultivated circles. So, illusory as that recognition might be, it was such a pleasant experience that I simply couldn't turn up my nose at it. Even if I knew that, at the time, a movie star could conquer Parisian society with nothing but his good looks. At the time the doors of Paris drawing rooms must have opened for many a young Greek or Yugoslav.

Those sophisticated ladies, some of whom were highly educated, went crazy over young fellows whose chief asset consisted of being aesthetically pleasing. I was young, good-looking (why be modest?), and had an exotic quality that intrigued women. I'd portrayed some little-known Arab who had become one of the most mysterious characters in world literature. Some of that must have rubbed off on me. And I'd come from a country that people talked about a great deal. There were the Pyramids and Farouk's tirades, but the rest . . . At times I felt like a gentle barbarian but didn't turn up my nose at fun.

People I didn't know (as well as some whose names were known everywhere) sent me invitations. Like Simone de Beauvoir. She once invited me to dinner at a château one hour from Paris. I'll never forget that gathering—the extraordinary setting, the sophisticated and important guests. I listened to them talk, I drank in their words. Without a doubt they roused my curiosity more than I did theirs. They were the ones putting on a show—not I. But how do we ever know who's the actor and who's the audience?

About that same time I met Françoise Sagan for the first time. I'm a sociable person, so I tend to go out a lot—especially when people give me a warm welcome. I joined Paris' nocturnal set, which gathers in fashionable discotheques like the Castel and the Régine. The drawing rooms attract people who come more for chatting than for dancing. And among these was Françoise Sagan, who was there almost every night. Me too. Françoise didn't talk much, but she was an admirable listener. I told stories that seemed quite dull to me, but Françoise—with a few sentences—would make them interesting. She had a gift for punctuating what other people said. Was it because she didn't want to "talk out" her stories that she listened so attentively to theirs?

I was quite fond of Françoise Sagan and yet I never read any of her books (except the screenplay made from *Bonjour Tristesse*). I knew her to be so reticent that I'm almost afraid of finding her there in her books. I also have the idea (mistaken perhaps) that she was writing for women.

Françoise gave me the impression of being perpetually unsatisfied, perpetually searching for something—an Ava Gardner, a Rita Hayworth with a French twist. I used to see a lot of her and really enjoyed her company but never felt like reading her. I've got to admit that I still prefer to dip into my boyhood favorites: Daudet, Maupassant, Anatole France, Proust, Camus. Poetry, too, with a marked preference for the romantics. What a wonderful use of language! I can't express an opinion on the contemporary poets. I haven't read them.

When it comes to reading, I'm very fortunate—I have insomnia, so I read a great deal. Until the wee hours of the morning. I wake up late, something that helps me get into the swing of Parisian life.

Often invited, I sometimes reciprocate. Either with some

motive or just for the fun of it. Motive? Well, to stay with a set in which I want to belong. For the fun? Because I have a good time when I'm with people. I don't overdo snobbish parties. When I go to any gathering I look for (and find) interesting, worth-while people who bring me certain things that I couldn't get within myself.

I'm a badly informed gentleman who makes no effort to keep abreast of world affairs on a daily basis. At these luncheons I can easily fill in any gaps in my political knowledge. There, from "well-informed" people I hear things you can't find in the papers. Effortlessly, I learn about things and have the pleasant impression of seeing what's going on behind the scenes in politics. I see the news being made.

I remember one dinner with Maurice Schumann who, as France's Minister of Foreign Affairs, maintained good relations with the Arab governments. On that particular evening he let me in on a thing or two about my brethren.

These dinners have also been the occasion of some juicy discoveries. I was recently invited to a dinner where I sat at the same table with the Duchess of Bedford. Our hosts belonged to the elite of Gotha, in West Germany, and it was clear that the duchess was shocking them by her straightforward way of talking. But her words had come from the lips of a duchess and it's the proper thing to applaud duchesses. . . . Had those same words come from the mouth of a plebeian they would have caused a scandal. They certainly hadn't been acceptable in that society. Titles —like wealth—make people bold.

I was in Milan for a bridge tournament about two years ago. I'd been invited to a billionaire's home. He and his wife welcomed me to their palatial mansion right in the heart of Milan, a mansion whose grounds they had extended by buying up (then, demolishing) adjacent buildings.

They talked about their hunting estate, another mansion,

near the airport a few miles outside Milan; in my honor,
they organized a festival there on the theme of hunting. On
the appointed day some thirty guests, big manufacturers
from northern Italy, showed up in elegant costumes. The
women were dressed in leopard skin or other equally expensive hides, and so were the men. All these outfits had been
specially tailored for the party.

I particularly recall one lady disguised as a falconer and
carrying a live falcon on her shoulder. The guests strolled
around chatting while an orchestra, brought all the way
from Monte Carlo, provided background music. The décor
was grandiose. Sixty white-wigged lackeys wearing seven-
teenth-century livery lighted the grounds with their torches.
The table had been set up under the elm trees that held the
cool of the night. The china was delicately glazed, artisti-
cally decorated. The cut glass and the heavy silverware
gleamed in the wavering flames of the torches. The wines
and food were extraordinary. The height of elegance and
refinement.

When the orchestra struck up music for dancing the
gentlemen, seated, began dozing off. Gaily, the ladies began
to dance with one another. Attentively, the hostess tried to
shake the men out of their torpor by inviting them to smash
the dishes.

China flew every which way before littering the ground.
The table was cleared away in less time than it takes to
write about it. The hostess called for more dishes, and the
lackeys appeared before each guest, loaded down with
white piles which would soon lie in fragments with the
other broken dishes.

I thought I was back with the tsars of old Russia, the ones
I'd read about in novels. When the guests ran out of china
they started in on chairs—period furniture—which the servants brought from inside. They smashed the chairs to bits,

then made a bonfire out of them . . . under the lackeys'
impassive eyes.

We weren't back with the tsars—this was something
straight out of Alfred Jarry's *Ubu-Roi*. The Parisian playwright hadn't made it up: the stupid vulgarity of a certain
class of wealthy people has no bounds.

Each chair sacrificed in that holocaust represented one
hundred times, a thousand times more than the monthly
wages of the people who were handing them over to the idi-
ocy of their masters.

I'm used to eccentricities, to the whims of billionaires, so I
shouldn't be shocked. But on that night I was. By those two
worlds: one shameless for its excesses, the other shameless
for its submissiveness. The destruction of valuable objects is
always shocking. But to destroy works of art in front of the
poor smacks of a challenge, even if the destroying party is
unaware of it. There's something intolerable about the rich
challenging the poor.

15.

I SAID THAT PARIS ADOPTED ME TWICE. The second time was when I was invited to Georges Pompidou's Thursday dinner parties. That was something of an official adoption, so I felt right at home.

And there was one other factor: the charm of Parisian women. American and British women (just to mention those two) are better-looking. The women you see in the streets of New York or London are, all things considered, more beautiful than Frenchwomen. But the Frenchwoman has charm.

What is this charm of hers? An attitude to men, to love, to the male-female relationship. It appears in her behavior with her mate, the way she talks to him, her tact, her knowhow.

The Englishwoman lacks this charm because it isn't in the manual of the perfect lady; the American woman lacks it because her matriarchal society doesn't allow her to take (or even pretend to take) a back seat to a sex that's called the weaker sex nowadays.

The Frenchwoman loves love—without self-consciousness, without untoward vanity, without thinking that she must be strong, stronger than the gentleman who is her mate, whether it's for one night, for a lifetime, for a weekend. The male within me delights at this, knowing that the most intel-

lectual woman, the smartest businesswoman, will put aside
her fine theories or her lucrative annual reports for me.

They say that Frenchwomen are changing. Maybe. In her
words. Let the ones who do all the shouting (it's easy to say
that they're frustrated) keep in mind that there are no ugly
women. There are only women who don't know how to be
pretty. La Bruyère must have said that.* And then, let's not
be afraid of generalizations: there's no woman in the world
who dresses better than the Parisian woman. Personally, I'm
ready to go on record, and the future will bear me out: if I
do remarry (and I thought about it seriously when I moved
to Paris) it will be a Frenchwoman. Or else I'll find a
woman elsewhere who convinces me that she has all the at-
tributes of a Frenchwoman.

So in 1969 I was thinking about marrying again, but
along came the bad days the astrologer had predicted.

What happened? Was my star on the wane? No. I'd
earned plenty of money, so much that I had to invest it. I
even hired a man I could trust to manage my assets, which
were placed in the New York Stock Exchange and in real estate. My investments exceeded my liquid assets and the accounts showed millions of francs. . . .

. . . My buildings had barely been completed when the
American stock market collapsed. The bottom dropped out
of real estate; interest rates went up; my horses, for which
I'd paid handsomely, turned out to be mediocre.

For the first time in my life I had money trouble. I had to
work to pay interest, to reimburse the banks, but the American motion picture industry was in hot water. . . . Everything was going wrong.

That's when the other phase of the predictions came true

---

* Jean de La Bruyère (1645–96), French essayist who wrote about the
follies and foibles of men and women. *Trans.*

—the phase concerning my character. The astrologer had spoken of an evolution of personality, reaching maturity. I'd never had to face any setbacks, either material or emotional, and suddenly, without being prepared for it, I had to cope with a situation that might become critical. These concerns led me to maturity, to an evolution of my personality.

I became aware of the value of money. I realized that I could have problems that were hard to solve. I became aware of certain real values that, up to then, I'd neglected in some dusty corner of my brain: friendship, family. I'd been accustomed to gambling twenty, thirty, even fifty million francs in a night. After all, what did those sums mean to me? A week's salary! I'd been behaving like movie stars of the twenties who squandered fortunes earned too easily. I had the impression that I was being given huge sums of money to gamble with . . . and I gambled it, all right!

What was I supposed to do—put a movie career in the same boat with blue-collar work? That's idiotic. What I made in one week most manual laborers couldn't make in a lifetime.

So I changed.

I stopped gambling. I took root at home, in Paris, in my own apartment, I went to a bridge club—always the same one—where I would be with the same people, who became my friends.

A new way of life opened up for me, a more normal way of life that enabled me to further my career at a pace I'd set for myself. Four pictures in two years, a fifth this year! That's a quota I never want to exceed.

The Tamarind Seed, a romantic spy story, enabled me to meet a happily married woman, an uncomplicated woman who plays the role of Mary Poppins in real life—Julie Andrews.

Terror on the Titanic is a suspense movie in which the

characters have only a certain degree of importance. The plot is everything. The part of the vessel's captain put me in a mariner's uniform for the first time, under the direction of Richard Lester, the man who did the American version of *The Three Musketeers*.

Once again, I was working with Barbra Streisand—this time in *Funny Lady*, the sequel to *Funny Girl*. Barbra, who'd been my wife in the first picture, has in this one remarried a theatrical producer, and her first husband (me) comes back into her life, just as she left him—wearing a tuxedo in a gambling casino.

This character resembled me a bit. We had been through a great love affair—both on and off the movie set. There we were, old friends getting together again—both on and off the set. She was thinking about her next picture. I wanted to get back to Austria, to another part, to a new movie adventure, with a new co-star. I'd picked her. She was Karen Black.

The film had been taken from a book by James Hadley Chase and was to be directed by an American I knew. A week before my departure for Austria—they phoned me to announce a change of directors. "It's going to be Ivan Passer." I'd never heard of him.

I put down the receiver and went back into the living room where I was chatting with Claude Chabrol. I must have had a nettled look, because he asked me if I'd just heard some bad news. I told him and he reassured me.

"That's terrific! I saw his last picture, *Law and Disorder*, in New York. It's on the list of the ten best American films for 1974. It's a huge success. I'd call Ivan Passer one of the best directors of our time."

So I went off confidently to Zürs, a little ski resort in the Arlberg region of Austria, and I wasn't disappointed. I met a real movie maker in the proper sense of the word, a leader of actors, a man who brought me out of myself. Here's what I mean by that.

In real life I conduct myself in a free and spontaneous way and, generally speaking, people like me. I found that the camera broke that natural spontaneity. Perhaps it was false modesty—the inability to let myself go all the way, to give myself up to the camera, a kind of paralysis.

Ivan Passer helped me find total freedom of expression. I did *Crime and Passion* without holding back. For the first time I let myself be expressed. It was fantastic. I have to admit that the part lent itself to this. It's a comedy—I have to make people laugh. Making audiences smile can be a wonderful thing. Which led me to the idea that I'd found a second career. I was only too happy to make this change, as I felt sure that the picture would be critically acclaimed.

Ivan Passer's sensitivity had a lot to do with it. Ivan is in the United States as a political refugee. A politically committed film maker in his own country, Czechoslovakia, he fled from the Russians in 1968. He'd had a brilliant debut with Milos Forman. Together, they won several prizes; together, they came as refugees to America; together, they conquered Hollywood before each went on to work in his own personal way.

Shooting a picture in Central Europe was a trial for Passer. He managed to phone his mother and son, who lived on the other side of the border, about twenty miles from Vienna. His mother begged him to come to the frontier.

"At least I'd be able to see you a hundred yards away, in a kind of shadow play."

Ivan may have reached his goal. He's awaiting American citizenship and will then be able to have his family brought over to the United States. I hope you make it, Ivan.

"In 1975, I can even be more exact—in the spring of 1975, there will be a new start." That's what the astrologer had said. Well, the spring of 1975 brought me more offers than I could accept—ten of them, one as enticing as the others. The future is clear.

What about afterward?
Afterward? There's hope—permanent hope of reaching perfection. But careers never quite turn out the way we want. They happen the way they have to happen, and there's nothing we can do to change it.
Outside of the cinema, I expect life to give me my daily game of bridge and colts that become champions.
I look forward to my son making progress in the direction he'd like to move. I'll help him reach his goal, whatever it is.
I hope to go on expanding my circle of friends and devote increasingly more time to my family.

Actually, I want today to be like yesterday. . . . Is that asking too much?

77

681578

681578

B
Sharif

Sharif, Omar, 1932-
   The eternal male / by Omar Sharif,
with Marie-Thérèse Guinchard ;
translated from the French by Martin
Sokolinsky. 1st ed. Garden City, N.Y. :
Doubleday, 1977.
   vii, 184 p., [8] leaves of plates :
ill. ; 22 cm.
   Translation of L'éternel masculin.

   1. Sharif, Omar, 1932-
2. Moving-picture actors and actresses
--Egypt--Biography. I. Guinchard,
Marie Thérèse, joint author. II. Title

GA   10 MAR 78   3272717 GAPApc   77-89418